The General Educator's Guide to Special Education

A Resource Handbook for All who Teach Students with Special Needs

Jody L. Maanum

Peytral Publications, Inc.

Minnetonka, MN   55345

Publisher's Cataloging-in-Publication
(Provided by Quality Books, Inc.)

Maanum, Jody L.
      The general educator's guide to special education : a
resource handbook for all who work teach students with
special needs / Jody L. Maanum. -- 2nd ed.
      p. cm.
      Includes bibliographical references and index.
      LCCN 2001132434
      ISBN 1890455350

1. Children with disabilities--Education--United
States--Handbooks, manuals, etc. 2. Special education--
Handbooks, manuals, etc. I. Title.

LC4019.M215 2004   371.9
                             QBI03-200796

Printed in the United States of America

Published by:
Peytral Publications, Inc.
PO Box 1162
Minnetonka, MN   55345-0162
Tel: 1-877-PEYTRAL (739-8725)
www.peytral.com

Table of Contents

Acknowledgements

I would like to thank Deanne Borgeson, for willingly leading my committee and for advising, supporting, and assisting me through the final phase of my Master's program. She is my mentor.

To Linda Svobodny, Brian Smith and John Benson, members of my committee for understanding the need for and allowing me to create this resource.

To Heidi Krause, my colleague and friend, for her countless hours of reading and re-reading this resource in an attempt to keep me focused.

To Dr. Thelma Anderson, my amazing grandma, for her grammatical expertise and words of praise and encouragement. I will always look to her with admiration.

To all of my students – past, present, and future – who have and continue to teach, motivate, and challenge me to be the best I can be.

To my parents, siblings, and family for their love, patience, and never-ending encouragement. I am blessed with you, my family.

Finally, to my husband and best friend, Joel, and my children Lacee Jo and Jaden Joel for their confidence, support, encouragement, and patience throughout this entire process. This accomplishment became reality because of you.

Section I

Definitions of Special Education Disability Categories

Special Education Disability Categories

The Individuals with Disabilities Act, IDEA, is a federal law that regulates all special education services in the United States. IDEA provides some federal funding to state and local education agencies to guarantee appropriate special education and related services for students who meet the criteria for eligibility. Currently, 13 separate disability categories are recognized under which students may be determined eligible to receive special education and related services.

<u>The 13 qualifying categories are:</u>
1. Autism
2. Deaf-blindness
3. Deafness
4. Emotional disturbance
5. Hearing impairment
6. Mental retardation
7. Multiple disabilities
8. Orthopedic impairment
9. Other health impairment
10. Specific learning disability
11. Speech or language impairment
12. Traumatic brain injury
13. Visual impairment including blindness

Following are descriptions of the thirteen qualifying categories. Specific examples of medical conditions which fall within these categories as well as possible educational approaches to working with children are also provided where appropriate.

Autism

Autism also referred to as Autism Spectrum Disorder (ASD) and/or Pervasive Developmental Disorder (PDD) is a developmental disability that affects a child's ability to communicate, understand language, play, and interact with others. Autism is a behavioral syndrome, which means that its definition is based on the pattern of behaviors that a child exhibits. Autism is not an illness or a disease and is not contagious. It is a neurological disability that is presumed to be present from birth and is always apparent before the age of three. Although autism affects the functioning of the brain, the specific cause is unknown. It is widely assumed that there are multiple causes, each of which may be manifested in different forms.

There are six frequently observed characteristics of children with autism.

1. Apparent Sensory Deficit.
Children with autism often appear not to see or hear things that are directed toward them. Even when the proximity is directly in front of the child, the child still may not react as if anyone is communicating with him or her.

2. Severe Affect Isolation.

This is noticed when someone attempts to love, cuddle, or show affection to the child. The child may respond with a profound lack of interest and will often push away from the attempt of affection.

3. Self-Stimulation.

Children with autism will often exhibit repetitive stereotyped acts, such as rocking when in a sitting or standing position, twirling around (often on tip toes), flapping hands, or humming a tune over and over again. They often become engrossed in staring at lights or spinning objects that seem to capture their attention.

4. Tantrums and Self-Mutilatory Behavior.

It is noted that children with autism may bite themselves until the bite draws blood, or will beat their heads against walls or furniture so hard that large lumps or bruises appear on the skin. A child may beat his or her face with fists, or even direct his or her aggression outward toward others by biting, kicking, and scratching. Once a child begins such a rage, it is difficult for parents or other adults to know how to handle and cope with these behaviors.

5. Echolalic and Psychotic Speech.

Many children with autism are mute, meaning they do not speak words or use communicable language, but may hum or utter simple sounds. Sometimes the speech of those who do speak will echo what other people are saying to them. For example, when a child is asked "What is your name?" the child may respond with "What is your name?" The echolalia (echoing someone else's words) is not immediate but delayed. The child may also repeat things such as television commercials, programs, or information heard in the past.

6. Behavior Deficiencies.

Along with the behaviors described above, there are many behaviors that are not exhibited by an autistic child that would be in a non-autistic child. By the age of 5 or 10, autistic children may show behavioral abilities of a 1-year-old child. They often exhibit few to no self-help skills, and need to be fed and dressed by others. These children often show no understanding or fear of common dangers. To help better understand autism, it should be noted that there are five disorders listed under the term Autism Spectrum Disorder (ASD) or Pervasive Developmental Disorder (PDD). The five disorders listed are Autistic disorder, Asperger's, Childhood Disintegrative Disorder, PDD-NOR (Pervasive Developmental Disorder Not Otherwise Specified), and Rett's.

There is tremendous confusion with the terms used to describe the disorder. Doctors will often use the term Autism Spectrum Disorder or Pervasive Developmental Disorder in the initial diagnosis as further evaluations will lead to a more conclusive diagnosis.

Pervasive Developmental Disorder-Not Otherwise Specified (PDD-NOS)

This is probably the most common category within PDD. PDD-NOS is generally used to mean "mild autism", or "some autistic characteristics" and is sometimes referred to as "atypical autism." This term refers to children who have significant difficulties in the area of social interaction, verbal communication (speech), nonverbal communication (gesture, eye contact), and play, but do exhibit some social characteristics which would indicate that they are not fully autistic.

Autistic Disorder

Children who are diagnosed in this category will exhibit significant difficulty in social interaction, language use, nonverbal communication (e.g., eye contact; gesture), pretend play, and will have a restricted range of interests. This diagnosis is less common than PDD-NOS. There are several specific symptoms that children must show in order to meet the criteria for autistic disorder. About 75% of children with autism also have mental retardation (are significantly delayed in all areas of understanding), while 25% of children with autism have normal intelligence except in areas related to language, social, and play development.

Asperger's Disorder (Asperger Syndrome)

Asperger's disorder refers to children who have ASD as described above (severe difficulty in social interaction and verbal and nonverbal communication, have a narrow range of interests and repetitive behaviors) but exhibit normal language and cognitive development. Sometimes the term "high functioning" children with autism has been used to describe this group of children.

Rett's Disorder (Rett's Syndrome)

Rett's disorder is an extremely rare medical condition that has only been reported in females. It has been added to the Autism Spectrum Disorder category because in addition to the medical symptoms, children with Rett's disorder tend to display social, communication, and play difficulties associated with ASD. The physical development of children with Rett's disorder is very distinct. Children have normal prenatal and perinatal development with typical early motor growth and head circumference. Between 5-30 months of age, mental and physical breakdowns begin to appear. Loss of muscle tone (hypotonia) is usually one of the first symptoms. Before long, the child will lose communication skills and the purposeful use of hands followed by the onset of perseverating hand-wringing movements. Rapid deterioration of gross motor skills will develop causing difficulty with crawling, walking, and very poor coordination.

Childhood Disintegrative Disorder (CDD)

Childhood Disintegrative Disorder (CDD) is an extremely rare condition. With CDD the child develops normally in all areas. Between the ages of 2-10 the child begins to lose previously learned skills. The loss of skills may include social, motor, and language skills as well as bowel and bladder control. Although children with other forms of ASD may exhibit the loss of skills as mentioned previously, the degree and extent of loss for children with CDD is more severe and pronounced.

Educational Approaches for Autism

Children with autism require and strive for structure and consistent scheduling. This helps the child to understand what is currently occurring and what is about to happen in the near future. This will also help the child to remain calm and not become as easily upset or agitated when schedule change occurs. Structure and schedules that are followed consistently help the child to learn as well as to become more independent.

Physical Structure is the way the classroom is set up and organized. A child with autism needs clear physical and visual boundaries in the classroom environment. Minimizing visual and auditory distractions is also important to help the child focus on learning concepts and not irrelevant details. The child also needs to know the basic teaching areas of the room. There should be specific designated areas that the child uses daily for a snack, play time, and transition times, as well as individual and independent work times. Theses areas should be consistent so there are no "surprises" in the child's routine. If a child with autism is accustomed to having a snack on the carpeted area at the front of the room every day, and suddenly is expected to eat a snack at his desk, this will likely cause agitation. Children with autism require consistency in all aspects of their day.

Daily Schedules are essential. Visual schedules help the child to see what activities will occur and the order of events for the day. The child will work best if a concrete reference of the daily schedule is in view. This will help the child to better accept change and become a bit more flexible, as long as the child knows in advance of a schedule change. A fire drill, for example, may be a devastating addition to the day, since the child is unaware that it will occur. In the eyes of an autistic child, if an event is not written on the schedule, then the event should not occur. Helping the child to become aware of upcoming event changes will ensure easier transition times when those events occur.

Visual Structure helps children with autism to capitalize on their visual aptitude and strengths and minimize their deficits in auditory processing. Visually highlighting important information will help to clarify the relevant concepts of which the child should be aware. This may include color-coding areas and labeling things to visually draw the child's attention. Providing visual instructions for the child is also helpful when presenting the child with an assignment or task.

It is important to remember that a child with autism needs consistency and structure. It is difficult for the child to be flexible without prior notice of a change in scheduling. If a child with autism does become upset, it is not because the child is naughty or bad. Often the child is upset because he is unaware of a change and is unable to handle or cope with the changes as his peer group can.

Deaf-Blindness

Deaf-Blindness is a medically verified hearing impairment coexisting with a medically verified visual impairment. Together, these two impairments must cause severe communication difficulties and other developmental and educational problems that cannot be accommodated in special education programs solely for children with exclusive blindness or deafness.

Deafness

Deafness is a hearing impairment so severe that the child cannot understand what is being said even with a hearing aid. The causes of a child being or becoming deaf are described in terms of exogenous or endogenous. Exogenous causes stem from factors outside the body such as disease, toxicity, or injury. Endogenous hearing impairments are genetic.

Educational Approaches for Children who are Deaf

Today, more than 60% of deaf children in the United States attend local school programs, and many are included in the regular classroom at least part of the day. Deafness does not affect a person's intellectual capacity or ability to learn, however, children who are deaf generally require some form of special education services in order to receive adequate instruction. The most difficult problem in educating deaf students is teaching spoken language to children who cannot hear. Many deaf students are not able to communicate effectively with classmates and therefore benefit by having a sing language interpreter to assist with the communication barrier. It is important for teachers and audiologists to work together to teach the child to use his or her residual hearing to the maximum extent possible, even if the preferred means of communication is manual.

Emotional Disturbance (ED)

An emotional disturbance refers to an established pattern characterized by one or more of the following behavior clusters:

a. Severely aggressive or impulsive behaviors
b. Severely withdrawn or anxious behaviors, general pervasive unhappiness, depression, wide mood swings
c. Severely disordered thought processes manifested by unusual behavior patterns, atypical communication styles, and distorted interpersonal relationships

This may include children with schizophrenic disorders, affective disorders, anxiety disorders, or other sustained disorders of conduct or adjustment when an established pattern adversely affects educational performance and results in either an inability to build or maintain satisfactory interpersonal relations necessary to the learning process. It should be noted that the established pattern of behavior must occur to a marked degree and over a long period of time.

The criteria for a child to be eligible for special education services in the area of emotional or behavior disorders states that the categories may include but are not limited to the medically diagnosed disorders listed and described below.

Schizophrenia

Schizophrenia is a psychosis or impairment of thinking in which the interpretation of reality and of daily events is severely abnormal. Signs of schizophrenia include delusions, prominent hallucinations for much of the day, incoherence, lack of or inappropriate display of emotions, and bizarre delusions (such as talking with people who do not exist). A person may also exhibit problems or decreased ability to function in work or participate in social interactions, and they may not exhibit appropriate personal hygiene. Schizophrenia usually appears during adolescence or early adulthood. The cause is unknown; however, many believe that it is an inherited disorder.

Treatment of Schizophrenia

Treatment of schizophrenia includes pharmacotherapy (medications) using antipsychotic medications, such as Risperdal, Risperidone, and Haldol (three of the many prescribed medications) combined with psychosocial interventions. The psychosocial interventions include supportive therapy with family, educational interventions, and vocational rehabilitation when appropriate.

Affective Disorders

Manic-Depressive Illness: (Bi-polar)

Bi-polar is an alternating pattern of emotional highs and high-spirited behavior (manic) and emotional lows (depression). The manic episodes and depressive episodes may alternate rapidly every few days. The mood swings experienced by one with this illness is unlike the mood swings that most people experience. Extreme and unpredictable mood swings from highly excited euphoria to the darkest depths of despair and depression are likely to be experienced by those affected by bi-polar disorder. The elation and depression occurs without relation to the circumstances. It is common to experience two or more complete cycles (a manic episode with a major depression episode with no period of remission) within a year.

Treatment of Bi-polar

Treatment of Bi-polar disorder is most effective through the use of medications, such as Lithium and Neuroleptics, along with psychosocial therapy. This would include intense patient-therapist interactions as well as family therapy.

Depression

A major depressive disorder is not simply sadness or grief, but is a genuine psychiatric illness that affects both the mind and body. Those who are depressed tend to retreat from human relationships, have trouble functioning in society, appear to be unable to enjoy life, and may even feel suicidal. Physical symptoms may include hollowness around eyes, uninflected speech, and a slowed pace. When one is nearing depression, there will be a change in physical demeanor. Lack of response to environmental changes, fatigue or loss of energy, poor appetite, insomnia, and suicidal behavior are all warning signs of clinical depression.

Treatment of Depression

Treatment for depression involves a multifaceted approach. Psychosocial intervention, such as family and individual therapy coupled with pharmacotherapy (medication) interventions such as Wellbutrin, Imipramine, Trazodone, and Effexor (some of the many medications used to treat depression) have been found to be effective.

Seasonal Affective Disorder (SAD)

Seasonal affective disorder (SAD) is a depression caused by a specific season of the year, most often winter. Some behaviors which may be exhibited include headaches, irritability, low energy level, and crying spells. One with SAD may tend to sleep a great deal in the winter and may gain weight. The cause is not known and usually begins in adolescence or young adulthood. The depression experienced by people who have SAD is much more significant than the gloomy dullness felt by many people during the winter months. This disorder is one that is not taken seriously by many people.

Treatment of Seasonal Affective Disorder

SAD can be treated with antidepressant medications as well as a special designed heat and light lamp.

Anxiety Disorders

Generalized Anxiety Disorder

Generalized anxiety disorder (GAD) is a relatively common anxiety problem, affecting 3-4% of the population. People who struggle with this disorder tend to turn their daily life into a state of worry, anxiety and fear by thinking and dwelling excessively on the "what ifs". GAD does not usually cause people to avoid situations, nor do they experience a "panic attack." It's more a matter of *thinking and dwelling and worrying and thinking and dwelling and worrying* to the point where they are unable to shut their mind off to irritating and over-exaggerated thoughts of everyday events. Feelings of worry, dread, lack of energy, and a loss of interest in life are common. Many times there is no "trigger" or "cause" for these feelings and the person realizes these feelings are irrational. Nevertheless, the feelings are very real. At this point, there is no "energy" or "zest" in life and no desire to want to do much.

Treatment of Generalized Anxiety Disorder

Generalized anxiety has been shown to respond best to cognitive-behavioral therapy. With the help of a therapist, the person gradually learns to see situations and problems in a different perspective and learns the methods and techniques to use to alleviate and reduce anxiety. Sometimes medication is helpful in addition to therapy, but for many people it is not necessary. Research indicates that generalized anxiety is fully treatable and can be successfully overcome over the course of about three to four months if the person is motivated and works toward recover.

Obsessive / Compulsive Disorder (OCD)

Obsessive/Compulsive Disorder (OCD) is an anxiety disorder in which people suffer intensely from recurrent, unwanted thoughts (obsessions) and/or repetitive behaviors (compulsions) that they feel they cannot control. Repetitive behaviors such as hand washing, counting, checking, or cleaning are often performed with the hope of preventing obsessive thoughts or making them go away. Performing these so-called rituals however, provides only temporary relief, and not performing them markedly increases anxiety. Left untreated, obsessions and the need to carry out rituals can take over a person's life. Both adults and children can develop OCD.

Other illnesses that may be related to OCD are **trichotillomania** (the repeated urge to pull out scalp hair, eyelashes, eyebrows, or other body hair); .**body dysmorphic disorder** (excessive preoccupation with imaginary or exaggerated defects in appearance), and **hypochondriasis** (the fear of having, despite medical evaluation and reassurance, a serious disease).

Treatment of Obsessive/Compulsive Disorder

Treatment of OCD must be two-fold, including both psychotherapy (talk therapy) as well as medications. The anti-anxiety medications are used to relax and calm the body, giving the psychotherapy and opportunity to work. Neither treatment, in isolation, will be effective or successful.

Panic Disorder

People with panic disorder suffer unexpected and repeated episodes of intense, overwhelming terror for no apparent reason (panic attacks). Their fear may be accompanied by physical symptoms such as chest pain, heart palpitations, sweating, hot or cold flushes, trembling, dizziness, choking or smothering sensations and shortness of breath. Some people feel like they are being devoured by fear, having a heart attack, or going crazy. Panic attacks can occur at any time, even during sleep. An attack generally peaks within 10 minutes, but some symptoms may last much longer.

Treatment of Panic Disorder

Both medication and psychotherapy should be combined to form a very effective treatment program for panic disorder. Medications that may be prescribed may include but are not limited to a variety of anti-anxiety medications (see benzodiazepines) as well as antidepressants.

Phobia

A phobia is a persistent, irrational fear of something, either an object or a situation. This phobia produces a compelling desire to avoid the feared object or situation. One who has a phobia is unable to control his or her emotions and may try to avoid the object creating the phobia. There are some students who experience school phobias, and will try to avoid school at all costs.

Treatment of Phobia

The most effective treatment of phobias includes both pharmacotherapy as well as direct psychosocial therapy. Medications that may be prescribed may include but are not limited to Buspar or antidepressants such as Imipramine or Nortriptyline.

Post Traumatic Stress Disorder (PTSD)

PTSD is an anxiety disorder that can develop after exposure to a terrifying event or ordeal in which grave physical harm occurred or was threatened. Traumatic events that may trigger PTSD include violent personal assaults, natural or human-caused disasters, accidents, or military combat.

Treatment for Post Traumatic Stress Disorder

There are two main types of treatment often used in conjuncture with each other to treat PTSD: psychotherapy and medication. As with the other anxiety disorders it is very important to treat the whole problem and learning to work through the fear and anxiety is essential. While working with a psychotherapist, anti-anxiety medications or antidepressants are used to calm anxiety and stabilize mood while other self-care tools are learned.

Separation Anxiety Disorder

Separation anxiety disorder is described as excessive worry and fear about being apart from family members or individuals to whom a child is most attached. Children with separation anxiety disorder fear being lost from their family or fear something bad will happen to a family member if they are separated from them. Symptoms of anxiety or fear about being separated from family members must last for a period of at least four weeks to be considered a separation anxiety disorder.

Treatment for Separation Anxiety Disorder

Anxiety disorders can be effectively treated. The treatment should always be based on a comprehensive evaluation of the child and family. Treatment recommendations may include cognitive behavioral therapy (CBT) for the child, with the focus being to help the child or adolescent learn skills to manage the anxiety and to help him/her master the situations that contribute to the anxiety. Some children may also benefit from treatment with antidepressant or anti-anxiety medication to help them feel calmer while they are working through their psychotherapy. Medication alone is never considered the treatment of choice given the high likelihood of relapse for individuals who receive medication without psychotherapy.

Conduct Disorders

Conduct disorders are a group of behavioral and emotional problems in children and adolescents. These children have great difficulty following rules and behaving in a socially acceptable way. They are often viewed by others as being "bad" or delinquent rather than mentally ill. Children with conduct disorders may exhibit some of the following behaviors: aggression toward people or animals, destruction of property, deceitfulness, lying, stealing, or a serious violation of rules. Many children with conduct disorders also experience coexisting conditions such as mood disorders, anxiety, substance abuse, ADHD, or learning problems.

Treatment of Conduct Disorders

Treatment of children with conduct disorders can be challenging. It is essential that treatment is provided in a variety of settings. Oftentimes, the child's uncooperative attitude, fear, and distrust cause difficulty as well. Behavior therapy and psychotherapy are usually necessary to help the child appropriately express and control anger. Treatment is often very time-consuming and lengthy, as establishing new attitudes and behavior patterns take time.

Oppositional Defiance Disorder (ODD)

All children are oppositional from time to time, particularly when tired, hungry, stressed or upset and such behavior is a very normal part of development for two to three year olds and early adolescents. However, openly uncooperative and hostile behavior becomes a serious concern when it is so frequent and consistent that it stands out when compared with other children of the same age and developmental level and when it affects the child's social, family, and academic life. Behaviors frequently displayed may include excessive arguing with adults, active defiance, refusal to comply with adult requests, and rules, deliberate attempts to annoy or upset people, blaming others for his or her mistakes or misbehavior, easily annoyed by others, frequent anger and resentment, and saying mean and hateful things when upset. In children with Oppositional Defiance Disorder (ODD) there is an ongoing pattern of uncooperative, defiant, and hostile behavior toward authority figures that seriously interferes with the youngster's day-to-day functioning.

Treatment for Oppositional Defiance Disorder

Treatment of ODD is most often a multi-faced approach, involving not just the child, but the child and his or her family. Such programming may include parent training programs to help manage the child's behavior, individual psychotherapy to develop more effective anger management, family psychotherapy to improve communication, Cognitive-Behavioral Therapy to assist problem solving and decrease negativity, and social skills training to increase flexibility and improve frustration and tolerance with peers.

Hearing Impairment

Children receiving services for a hearing impairment generally exhibit difficulty with hearing, whether permanent or fluctuating, that adversely affects educational performance. Sound is measured by its loudness (measured in units called decibels, dB) and its frequency or pitch (measured in units called hertz, Hz). Impairments in hearing can occur in either or both areas, and may exist in only one ear or in both ears. Hearing loss is generally described as slight, mild, moderate, severe, or profound, depending upon how well a person can hear the intensities or frequencies most greatly associated with speech.

Educational Approaches for Hearing Impairments

Children who are hard of hearing will find it much more difficult than children who have normal hearing to learn vocabulary, grammar, word order, idiomatic expressions, and other aspects of verbal communication. Services that may be beneficial for children in educational setting may include: regular speech, language, and auditory training from a specialist; amplification systems; services of an interpreter for those students who use sign language; favorable seating in the class to facilitate lip reading; captioned films/videos; assistance of a note-taker so the student can fully attend to instruction; instruction for the teacher and peers in alternate communication methods, such as sign language and counseling.

Mental Retardation

This category refers to a condition resulting in significantly below-average intellectual functioning and concurrent deficits in adaptive behavior that adversely affect educational performance and require special education and related services. This category does not include conditions primarily due to sensory or physical impairments, traumatic brain injury, autism, severe multiple impairments, cultural influences, or inconsistent educational programming.

Mild to Moderate Range

For programming purposes once a student has met the eligibility criteria to receive special education and related services in the category of Mental Retardation, the student is placed into either the mild-moderate range or the severe-profound range. A student's intellectual functioning, as indicated by an intelligence quotient (IQ) below 70, is necessary in order for the student to be considered in the mild-moderate range. A student must also demonstrate a delay in adaptive functioning which is related to the student's personal independence and social responsibility.

Students with mild to moderate developmental cognitive disabilities make up 80 to 85% of the people identified in this category. For the majority of students with mild impairments, the cause is unknown. Although there is no direct evidence that social and familial interactions cause mental impairments, it is generally believed that these influences may have some effect on the mild cases of mental impairments.

Educational Approaches for Mild to Moderate Mental Retardation

The trend of educating students with mild-moderate mental retardation is changing. Traditionally, the students in the mild-moderate range were educated in self-contained classrooms with their peers. Today, increasing numbers of these students are spending more of their school day in the general education classroom with supplemental instruction provided by a resource teacher or a special education assistant. Simply placing a student into general education does not mean that the student will be immediately successful. Systematically planning for the student's integration into the classroom through team activities, group investigation projects, and directly training all students in specific skills for interaction with one another are just some of the methods

© *Peytral Publications Inc.*

that will help increase the chance of success in the general education setting. Peer tutoring has also proven to be very effective.

Many students in the mild-moderate range are educated in regular classrooms with extra support provided as needed. These students are generally able to master standard academic skills and often tend to plateau at approximately a sixth grade level. Students with moderate mental impairments are also frequently taught communication, self-help, daily living, and vocational skills in addition to limited academics.

Severe to Profound Range

Students who are placed into the severe-profound range within this category exhibit significantly sub-average general intellectual functioning resulting in or associated with concurrent deficits in adaptive behavior that may require special education instruction and related services. A student's intellectual functioning as indicated by an intelligence quotient (IQ) must be below 50 for the student to be placed into the severe-profound range. A student must also demonstrate a delay in his or her ability to be independent and socially responsible, which is considered a student's adaptive functioning.

<u>Educational Approaches for Moderate to Severe Mental Impairments</u>

The self-contained special education classroom is the most common educational placement for students with a severe-profound developmental cognitive disability, although the trend is changing and more students are placed in the general education setting for a portion of their school day.

Developing functional curriculum goals for these students is the primary goal for most educators. Curriculum choices include developing goals around the domains that represent the person as he or she lives, works, plays, and moves through the community. Personal maintenance and development, homemaking, community life, vocation, and leisure and travel are the five domains on which many curriculums for mentally impaired students are based.

One effective technique to use with students with severe-profound mental retardation is task analysis. This is a method in which large skills are broken down and sequenced as a series of smaller subtasks. The small, easier subtasks enable the student to learn easily and experience success more frequently. The subtasks are sequenced in the natural order in which they are performed. In spite of the severe mental impairment, these students are able to learn. The curriculum stresses function, communication, and self-help skills. If students are provided with repeated opportunities to respond and practice as well as positive reinforcement for appropriate behavior, they are much more likely to be successful.

Chromosome Abnormalities

Down Syndrome

Down syndrome is caused by the presence of an extra chromosome 21. It is common and occurs in approximately 1 in 900 births. Children with Down syndrome show some distinctive physical characteristics such as upwardly slanting eyes and small ears, nose, feet and hands, along with a flattened facial profile, short stature, a large tongue, and a gap between the first and second toes. Other characteristics of this syndrome are visual and auditory problems, thyroid disease, cardiac conditions, premature senility, loose ligaments, and decreased muscle tone. Due to low muscle tone, people with Down syndrome have a tendency to keep their mouths open. Low muscle tone coupled with a large tongue makes speech articulation more difficult. Mental retardation accompanies this syndrome but the level of intellectual ability varies. Cardiac problems are the major cause for concern of people with Down syndrome. Most people with Down syndrome function in the mild or moderate range of retardation.

Educational Approaches for Down Syndrome

Down syndrome is recognizable at birth, which allows for early intervention from a variety of professionals. Early intervention provides parent(s) with up-to-date information so the parent(s) can help the child get a head start on learning. Professionals involved in early intervention screening and follow-up may include physicians, speech and language professionals, audiologists, education specialists, and physical and occupational therapists. A strength that is commonly noted in people with Down syndrome is that they often have a pleasant disposition, and behavior problems are uncommon.

Fragile X Syndrome

Fragile X syndrome accounts for the most common inherited form of mental retardation. This syndrome is linked to an irregularity in the X chromosome and usually results in mental retardation in males and learning disorders in females. Physical characteristics of this syndrome include a prominent jaw and an enlarged head, ears, and testes (in males). The student may exhibit autistic-like behaviors such as withdrawal, heightened interest in sensations, stereotypical hand movements, behavior problems (hand biting), and hyperactivity.

Fragile X Syndrome is often difficult to diagnose during childhood. The physical characteristics may be minimal or not noticed until they become more pronounced following puberty. There is a slow regression in abilities over time.

Educational Approaches for Fragile X Syndrome

Early intervention is recommended so that physical therapy, speech and language therapy, and occupational therapy can be started. Positive behavioral strategies and medications have been used to improve problems of self injury and hyperactivity.

Hunter Syndrome

This condition is an X-linked syndrome that is genetically transmitted and affects only males, but it is carried by females. It is rare, as it occurs in approximately 1 in 50,000 births. Infants born with Hunter's syndrome show no immediate outward signs. During the first two years of life, some children may have excessive growth. The effects of Hunter's syndrome become quite apparent after the second year of life. At this time there is observable mental deterioration that can result in aggressive and hyperactive behaviors. Typical physical characteristics may include small stature, short neck, joint contracture, large head (hydrocephalus), broad, low nose, full cheeks, thick lips, and widely-spaced teeth. Impaired hearing usually begins later in childhood.

There are two types of Hunter's syndrome: Type A and Type B. Type A is also called juvenile type and is more severe than Type B. This type has rapid progression, resulting in severe mental retardation and death before 15 years of age due to liver and cardiac problems. Type B progresses much more slowly. There is slight or no noticeable mental impairment and people with Type B may live to be 50 or 60 years old.

Educational Approaches for Hunter Syndrome

The interventions necessary for a child with Hunter syndrome will depend on the type and severity of the symptoms. Early intervention is most helpful to address each individual's needs. Speech and language consultants can provide recommendations to enhance communication. Audiologists can assess and provide hearing devices for those with auditory problems. Surgery can be used to correct hernias, and shunting can be implemented to decrease pressure on the brain. Behavior management consultants or psychologists can provide guidance in decreasing aggressive behaviors, increasing productive expression of wants and needs, and managing hyperactivity.

Klinefelter Syndrome (47XXY)

This genetic disorder develops in males only. It occurs in approximately 1 in every 500-1000 male births. This syndrome is caused by an additional female X chromosome on the chromosome chain that determines gender. This additional X chromosome affects the production of testosterone which can result in the following physical characteristics: small testes, lack of facial hair, and breast development.

Some common features of people with this syndrome are increased height, poor upper body strength, delay in language development, and difficulty with auditory processing. Mental retardation is not a prominent feature of this syndrome as only 10-20% of people with Klinefelter syndrome have intelligence in the mild-moderate mental retardation range.

Fetal Alcohol Syndrome (FAS)

This syndrome is the leading cause of mental retardation and the second most common birth defect. It occurs in 1 in 600-700 births, and is 100% preventable. FAS is a condition characterized by physical and behavioral disabilities that occur because of exposure to alcohol prior to birth. The mother's use of alcohol during pregnancy is a criterion for diagnosis of these conditions. Children with FAS may be small and often have distinctive facial features. These may include the lack of a crease between the nose and upper lip, a flat nasal bridge, a thin upper lip, a small jaw, a small head, and/or eyes which are distinctive in shape, size, or position. Physical problems such as joint and limb malformations, heart problems, kidney disorders, and cleft lip/palate may be apparent. Mental impairment is also a feature of this syndrome and can include mental retardation, learning disorders, behavior problems, and gross motor limitations.

Problems stemming from this disorder can be seen in infancy. Babies with FAS are usually born small and underdeveloped. Behavioral concerns may consist of hyperactivity and a short attention span, and decreased physical abilities are commonly noted in pre-school and school-aged children.

Educational Approaches for Fetal Alcohol Syndrome

Early intervention increases the child's chances for later success. Early intervention provides a variety of assessments in the areas of physical and mental ability. Physicians, physical and occupational therapists, speech and language therapists, and people who specialize in child development can assess the child's strengths and abilities along with areas where additional support is needed. The best time for intervention to begin is shortly after birth.

Multiple Disabilities

The category called Multiple Disabilities involves severe learning and developmental problems resulting from two or more disability conditions determined by assessment. A student is eligible to receive service for severely multiply impaired if the student meets the entrance criteria for two or more of the following disabilities:

1. Hearing Impairment
2. Orthopedic Impairment
3. Mental Retardation
4. Visual Impairment
5. Emotional Disturbance
6. Autism

Orthopedic Impairment

The category of Orthopedic Impairment involves a severe impairment that may adversely affect a child's physical or academic functioning and result in the need for special education and related services. The category includes impairments caused by congenital abnormality (from birth), impairments caused by disease, and impairments from other causes. Examples of such orthopedic impairments which may require special education services may include but are not limited to those listed below.

Burns

Burns are the leading type of injury in childhood. Most often, burns result from household accidents but sometimes they are the result of child abuse. Serious burns can cause complications in other organs, long-term physical limitations, and psychological difficulties. Children with serious burn injuries usually experience pain, scarring, limitations of motion, lengthy hospitalizations, and repeated surgeries.

Educational Information about Burns

The disfigurement caused by severe burns can affect a child's behavior and self-image, especially if teachers and peers react negatively. When a child is returning to class after a prolonged absence resulting from an extensive burn injury, it may be advisable for the teacher, parents, or other involved persons to explain to classmates the nature of the child's injury and appearance.

Cerebral Palsy (CP)

Cerebral palsy is one of the most prevalent physical impairments in children. It is a long-term condition resulting from a lesion to the brain or an abnormality of brain growth. Cerebral palsy is a disorder in which muscular development and control are impaired. The significance of this injury and the effects vary for each person. The brain injury may occur prior to birth from a disease or injury to the mother during pregnancy, during a traumatic birth, or later in life as the result of an infection, disease, or head trauma.

There is no cure for CP; however, it can be treated. The impairment usually does not deteriorate as a child ages. It is not fatal or contagious. These children usually have disturbances of voluntary motor functions. This may include paralysis, extreme weakness, poor coordination, involuntary convulsions, and other motor disorders. They may have little or no control over their arms, legs, or speech, depending on the degree of the impairment. It is possible to have a hearing and/or vision impairment as well.

Educational Approaches for Cerebral Palsy

The use of assistive technology and adaptive equipment can help a person with CP cope with some of the physical limitations associated with this disability. Physical and occupational therapy will help to maintain good muscle quality. Some medication can be used to strengthen muscle groups as well. Speech therapy may be helpful if the muscles affecting speech are involved in the disability.

Duchenne's Muscular Dystrophy

This disorder is a progressive disease of muscle weakening and is the most common and severe form of childhood muscular dystrophy. It is genetically transmitted from the mother and affects only males. There are no physical characteristics of Duchenne's MD that make this syndrome noticeable at birth. A child with Duchenne's develops normally until the second to sixth year of life, when the onset of this disease is first seen. Early symptoms such as falling, walking on toes, and having a protruding abdomen and difficulty in running are often overlooked until more severe signs of this syndrome set in. There is a progressive weakening of the pelvis, upper arms, and upper legs. The use of a wheelchair may be required by ages 12-15. Physical therapy can help people with Duchenne's MD prolong their ability to walk. In the later stages of Duchenne's, the respiratory system is affected and breathing becomes difficult. This leads to an increased susceptibility to respiratory infections and pneumonia. Most people with Duchenne's MD have a life span of 20-30 years. Mental retardation is common with this syndrome.

Educational Approaches for Muscular Dystrophy

People with MD require support to maintain their physical health and independence. Intervention strategies include orthopedic support (wheelchairs, crutches, specialized beds), symptom treatment for infections, physical and occupational therapy to help maintain muscle condition, and possible surgery for muscle contractures. In school, a teacher should be careful not to lift a child with muscular dystrophy by the arms, as even a gentle pull may dislocate the child's limbs.

Limb Deficiency

A limb deficiency is the absence or partial loss of an arm or leg. A congenital limb deficiency or absence of a limb at birth is rare. Acquired limb deficiencies (amputations) are more common and are often the result of surgery or an accident.

Educational Information about Limb Deficiencies

Some students may use a prosthesis or artificial limb to assist with a variety of tasks and to create a more normal appearance. Some students, however, prefer not to use the prosthesis. Most children become quite proficient at using their remaining limbs. Some children who are missing both arms, for example, may need to re-learn different tasks and skills, such as learning to write with their feet. Unless children have other impairments in addition to the absence of limbs, they should be able to function in a regular classroom with only minor modifications.

Spina Bifida

Spina bifida is a term used to describe a neural tube defect that occurs anywhere along the spine. In the most common form of spina bifida – myelomeningocele – there is an opening in both the backbone (vertebrae) and the skin around it, so that the spinal cord protrudes through the back. The damaged spinal cord results in a loss of sensation and movement in some parts of the body. Usually, spina bifida results in problems with mobility and bowel and bladder control. Some evidence does support the possibility that spina bifida is inherited. Researchers have also recently shown a link between diet and this disorder. It has been found that a small amount of the B vitamin, folic acid, taken the month prior to conception and during the first several months of pregnancy, significantly reduces the chances of having a child with this birth defect.

There are three types of spina bifida. The first is called *occulta* and is a harmless form of spina bifida. It is possible that people who have this form will never even know that they have spina bifida. In this form, there is a small gap in the vertebrae of the back. The spinal cord and nerves are not affected and no problems are caused by this gap.

The second and rarest type is called *meningocele*. In this type, the protective membranes that surround the spine push out through an opening in the vertebrae, creating a cyst. The cyst can be small or large. The spinal cord remains intact and the cyst is surgically removed. There is usually no subsequent damage and the child can go on to lead a life without further spinal complications.

The third type of spina bifida is the most complicated and severe. This type is called *myelomeningocele*. This occurs when a portion of the spinal cord protrudes through the back. Often the cord is exposed and lacking spinal fluid. The cord may be covered with sores and is extremely prone to infection. Surgery to seal the opening is usually performed within the first 48 hours of life, but many complications still result. At the site of the exposed cords, and below, the child has paralysis. Because the nerves that control bowel and bladder functions are located very low on the spinal cord, 95% of people with this form of spina bifida will not have control of their bowels and bladder. Due to the damage to the spinal cord, there are usually problems with the flow of spinal fluid from the brain, which can result in a build up of fluid in the brain. This fluid can cause brain damage if not drained, so a shunting procedure is surgically performed to drain the excess fluid into other body cavities.

Educational Approaches for Spina Bifida

Early intervention is important for a child with spina bifida. Physical therapists, occupational therapists, neurologists, neurosurgeons, orthopedists, pediatricians, nutritionists, psychologists, and nurses can help to plan for and implement strategies to enable the person with this syndrome to be as comfortable and independent as possible. These children will usually walk with braces, crutches, or a walker, and they may use wheelchairs for longer distances.

Other Health Impairment (OHI)

The Other Health Impairment (OHI) category includes a broad range of medically diagnosed chronic or acute health conditions that may adversely effect academic functioning and result in the need for special education instruction and related services. The decision that a specific health condition qualifies under the OHI criteria will be determined by the impact of the condition on academic functioning rather than by the diagnostic or medical label given the condition.

To be deemed eligible for special education services in the area of OHI there must be a medically diagnosed chronic or acute health condition that affects academic functioning. Examples of these medically diagnosed chronic or acute health conditions include but are not limited to the examples listed below.

ADD/ADHD

Attention Deficit Disorder (ADD)

Attention Deficit Disorder describes a child who has difficulty with maintaining attention but is not hyperactive. ADD can be very difficult and problematic for a child. Children with ADD are generally not disruptive in the classroom and their behaviors are usually not noticeable or distracting to others. ADD can cause a child to underachieve in the classroom and have low self-esteem. Some behavioral characteristics of a child with ADD may include being easily distracted by extraneous stimuli, having difficulty listening and following directions, having difficulty focusing and sustaining attention, having difficulty concentrating and attending to task, showing inconsistent performance on school work, being disorganized (can't find paper, pencils, books), having poor study skills, and struggling to work independently.

Attention Deficit Disorder with Hyperactivity (ADHD)

Attention Deficit Disorder with Hyperactivity describes a child who has the components as mentioned above in addition to a hyperactivity component. Along with all the characteristics described above, the child with the hyperactivity component will also exhibit a high activity level (in constant motion, fidgeting with hands or feet, falling from chair), impulsivity, lack of self-control (blurts out, can't wait for turn, interrupts, talks excessively), difficulty with transitions/changing activities, aggressive behavior, social immaturity, low self-esteem, and high frustration.

Educational and Medical Approaches for ADD/ADHD

Treatment of ADD/ADHD must include a multifaceted approach. It may include behavior modification at home and school, counseling, cognitive therapy (stop and think techniques), social skills training, provision of a physical outlet, parent education, and pharmacotherapy or medications. There are many medications found useful in treating ADD/ADHD. Medications include but are not limited to stimulants such as Ritalin, (methylphenidate, generic of Ritalin), Dexedrine, Cylert, Adderall, and Tofranil (imipramine, generic of Tofranil).

Asthma

Asthma is characterized by episodes of narrowing of the bronchial tubes in the lungs. Normally, these tubes narrow only as a protective reaction to prevent harmful substances from entering the lungs. With asthma, the bronchial tubes narrow too much, too often, and too easily in response to a variety of substances that ordinarily would not damage the lungs. Signs and symptoms of asthma include shortness of breath, coughing, tightness of the chest, and wheezing.

Medical and Educational Approaches for Asthma

Asthma is one of the most frequently cited reasons for missing school. Chronic absenteeism makes it difficult for the child with asthma to maintain performance at grade level. Most children who receive medical and psychological support are able to successfully complete school and lead normal lives. Treatment of asthma is most often through medication dispersed using inhalers and nebulizers. An inhaler can be used periodically throughout the day when an asthmatic senses an attack or a need to clear the airway passages. A nebulizer is used for more severe instances of an asthma attack. Once children have been informed and are educated about their condition, they are often able to "feel" when they need to use their inhaler to proactively prevent an asthmatic attack from developing. Children with asthma need to be allowed to use their inhaler as necessary throughout the day.

Bronchopulmonary Dysplasia (BPD)

This is a chronic lung disease in which those infected experience persistent difficulty in breathing and abnormal changes on chest X-rays. In most cases, BPD occurs in infants who are born prematurely and who have Respiratory Distress Syndrome (RDS). BPD most often surfaces after babies have received extra oxygen and/or been on a mechanical ventilator to treat their original lung problem. It is possible that the symptoms of BPD can disappear rapidly; however, some infants with BPD may have breathing difficulties for many months or years. Some infants may depend on a mechanical ventilator throughout early childhood. BPD survivors are more susceptible to complications from normal childhood viruses and illnesses. Babies who survive BPD may also have a slower growth rate and may remain smaller than children of the same chronological age. Some may continue to have problems with lung function even when they are adults. The outlook for growth and development of babies with BPD varies. In severe cases, there may be some long-term limitations. These might include abnormalities in coordination, gait, and muscle tone, inability to tolerate exercise, vision and hearing problems, and learning disabilities. For the majority, however, few complications are noticed after early childhood.

Educational Approaches for Bronchopulmonary Dysplasia

For those children who exhibit limitations due to BPD when they reach school-age, special considerations need to be taken regarding the physical expectations and requirements of the child.

Chronic Fatigue Syndrome

Someone with chronic fatigue syndrome may suffer from persistent or relapsing fatigue that lasts six or more consecutive months. All other known diseases, infections, or psychiatric illnesses that might cause the following symptoms must be ruled out. A person with chronic fatigue syndrome must show evidence of at least four of the following eight symptoms. The symptoms include sore throat, painful lymph nodes in the neck or armpits, prolonged fatigue following previously tolerated exercise, new generalized headaches, unexplained muscle soreness, pain that moves from one joint to another without evidence of redness or swelling, impaired memory and concentration, and sleep disturbance.

Treatment of Chronic Fatigue Syndrome

Chronic fatigue syndrome is a syndrome of symptoms and in most cases there is no serious underlying disease causing it. There is no treatment for this syndrome. In most cases, doctors will treat the symptoms that develop due to the syndrome.

Cystic Fibrosis

Cystic fibrosis is an inherited disease that affects both the respiratory and the digestive systems. It is the most common fatal hereditary disease in Caucasian children. It occurs in boys and girls equally and is inherited on a recessive basis, which means that a child can have cystic fibrosis only if both parents are carriers of the disease. Cystic fibrosis affects the mucus and sweat glands of the body. As a child gets older, chronic respiratory disease may develop, including bronchitis, a collapsed lung due to blockage of airways, pneumonia, or fibrosis of the lung. Cystic fibrosis is very serious and ultimately fatal.

Treatment of Cystic Fibrosis

Treatment of cystic fibrosis is a long-term process, and frequent checkups are important. The child should be given a pancreatic enzyme to supply the missing digestive enzymes. There are also special exercises that parents can perform to loosen and promote drainage of the mucus. This involves tapping or pounding on the child's back several times each day to assist in loosening the mucus. Many children and young adults with this condition are able to lead active lives. With continued research and treatment techniques, the long-range outlook for children affected by cystic fibrosis is improving.

Cytomegalovirus (CMV)

Cytomegalovirus or CMV is a common virus, and most adults and children who contact this virus display no symptoms or problems. It is estimated, however, that approximately 1 percent of all newborns are infected with congenital CMV before birth, resulting in a serious disability in more than 4,000 children each year. In some cases children whose mothers were infected during pregnancy may have birth defects such as hearing loss, mental retardation, or delays in development.

Educational Approaches for Cytomegalovirus

Specific educational planning should be made for children with this severe form of CMV.

Diabetes

Diabetes is a disorder of metabolism that affects the way the body absorbs and breaks down sugars and starches in food. It is a common childhood disease and affects about 1 in 600 school-aged children. A child with diabetes will lack energy. Several important parts of the body, such as the eyes and kidneys, can be affected by untreated diabetes. Early symptoms of diabetes include thirst, headaches, loss of weight, frequent urination, and cuts that are slow to heal.

Medical and Educational Approaches for Diabetes

Children with diabetes have insufficient insulin, which is a hormone normally produced in the body. To regulate this condition, insulin must be injected into the body daily. A specific diet and a regular exercise program are usually suggested.

Teachers should be aware of the symptoms of insulin reaction, also called *diabetic shock*. It can result from taking too much insulin, from strenuous exercise, or from a missed or delayed meal. Symptoms of insulin reaction or diabetic shock include faintness, dizziness, blurred vision, drowsiness, and nausea. A child may appear irritable or have a marked personality change. In most cases, giving a child some form of concentrated sugar (sugar cube, a glass of fruit juice, or a candy bar) should end the reaction within a few minutes.

Epilepsy

Epilepsy is a seizure disorder that briefly interrupts the normal electrical activity of the brain, causing seizures. Seizures are characterized by a variety of symptoms including uncontrolled movements of the body, disorientation or confusion, or loss of consciousness. Epilepsy may result from a head injury, stroke, brain tumor, lead poisoning, genetic conditions, or severe infections like meningitis or encephalitis. In over 70 percent of cases, no cause for epilepsy is identified.

Seizures: Epileptic seizures vary in intensity and symptoms depend on what part of the brain is involved. Seizures are classified as simple partial, complex partial, absence seizures, and grand mal seizures (convulsions).

Simple partial seizures cause people to experience uncontrollable jerky motions of a body part, sight or hearing impairment, sudden sweating, nausea, and feelings of fear.

Complex partial seizures last for only one or two minutes. The person experiencing the seizure may appear to be in a trance and may move randomly with no control over body movements. This form of a seizure may be preceded by an "aura" or a warning sensation.

Absence seizures are characterized by a sudden, momentary loss or impairment of consciousness. Overt symptoms are often an upward staring of the eyes, a staggering gait, or a twitching of facial muscles. No aura occurs prior to the seizure. Following the seizure, the person resumes activity without realizing that the seizure has occurred.

Grand mal seizures involve the whole brain. This type of seizure is often signaled by an involuntary scream, caused by contraction of the muscles that control breathing. As loss of consciousness sets in, the entire body is gripped by a jerking muscular contraction. The face reddens, breathing stops, and the back arches. Subsequently, alternate contractions and relaxation of the muscles throw the body into sometimes violent agitation such that the person may be subject to serious injury. After the convulsion subsides, the person is exhausted and may sleep heavily. Confusion, nausea, and sore muscles are often experienced upon awakening, and the person may have no memory of the seizure. Attacks occur at varying intervals, in some people as seldom as once a year and in others as frequently as several times a day.

Medical and Educational Approaches for Epilepsy

There is no cure for epilepsy, but symptoms of the disorder may be treated. The majority of children with epilepsy can be helped with anticonvulsant medications such as Tegretol, Depakene, Depakote, or Klonopin. Medications can sharply reduce and even eliminate seizures in many cases. All children with epilepsy will benefit from a realistic understanding of their condition and from accepting and supportive attitudes on the part of teachers and classmates.

Hemophilia

Hemophilia is a blood disease that does not allow the blood to clot. It is caused by genes that are recessive and sex-linked (carried on the sex chromosome) so the disorder almost always occurs in boys, not girls. The major problem for people with hemophilia is not superficial external cuts but uncontrolled internal bleeding. Signs and symptoms of hemophilia include large or deep bruises, pain and swelling of joints, blood in the urine, and prolonged bleeding from cuts or injuries.

Medical and Educational Approaches for Hemophilia

Most people with hemophilia can live a relatively normal life. Exercise, medication, and, in some instances, surgery may be necessary to treat hemophilia. In school, a student may need to be excused from some physical activities and may need the use of a wheelchair during times he or she is experiencing difficulties.

Specific Learning Disabilities (SLD)

A Specific Learning Disability is defined as a condition within the individual affecting learning relative to potential.

1. A specific learning disability is manifested by interference with acquisition, organization, storage, retrieval, manipulation, or expression of information inhibiting the ability of the individual to learn at an adequate rate when provided with the usual developmental opportunities and instruction from a regular school environment.

2. A specific learning disability is demonstrated by a significant discrepancy between a student's general intellectual ability and academic achievement in one or more of the following areas: oral expression, listening comprehension, mathematical calculation, mathematical reasoning, basic reading skills, reading comprehension, or written expression.

3. A specific learning disability is demonstrated primarily in academic functioning, but may also affect self-esteem, career development, and life-adjustment skills. A specific learning disability may occur with but cannot be primarily the result of a visual, hearing, motor, or mental impairment; an emotional disorder; environmental, cultural, or economic influences; or a history of an inconsistent education program.

Educational Approaches for Learning Disabilities

There are two basic approaches to educating learning disabled children: ability training and skills training. Ability training includes instructional activities designed to remediate a child's weakness in underlying basic abilities.

Skill training is based on the belief that a child's performance deficit is the problem, not a sign of an underlying disability. In skill training, remediation is based on direct instruction of precisely defined skills, many opportunities for practice and repetition, and a direct measurement of a child's progress. Research has shown this approach to be effective.

Children with learning disabilities are educated in a variety of placements and receive many different delivery arrangements, but most students with learning disabilities are educated in the regular classroom for the majority of the school day. A consultant teacher may help the regular classroom teacher work with children with learning disabilities in the classroom, providing support and modifications of regular assignments.

The resource room may also be used to deliver service to children with learning disabilities. This would involve a specially trained teacher to work with the child on a particular skill deficit for one or more periods a day in a classroom away from the regular education classroom.

Apraxia

Speech or Language Impairment (SL)

Approximately 5% of school-aged children have a speech or language impairment that is serious enough to require special education services. Speech and language impairments may be divided into four separate categories: fluency disorder, voice disorder, articulation disorder, and language disorder. Nearly twice as many boys as girls have speech impairments. Children with articulation problems represent the largest category of speech/language impairments.

Although some speech disorders do have an organic cause, most disorders cannot be attributed to a physical condition. Speech and language impairments that can be attributed only to dialectical, cultural or ethnic differences or the influence of a foreign language should not be identified as a disorder.

Fluency Disorder

A fluency disorder is the intrusion of repetition of sounds, syllables, and words, prolongation of sounds, avoidance of words, silent blocks, inappropriate inhalation or exhalation, or problems with phonation patterns. These patterns may also be accompanied by facial and body movements associated with the effort to speak. The most common fluency disorder is stuttering.

Voice Disorder

A voice disorder is the absence of voice or presence of abnormal quality, pitch, resonance, loudness, or duration in one's voice.

Articulation Disorder

An articulation disorder is the absence of or incorrect production of speech sounds that are developmentally appropriate.

Language Disorder

A language disorder is a breakdown in communication as characterized by problems in expressing needs, ideas, or information and which may be accompanied by problems in understanding.

Educational Approaches for Speech and Language Impairments

Different types of communication disorders require different approaches to remediation. This is usually done one-on-one or in group settings with a specially trained speech and language pathologist. Most of the children with speech disorders attend regular classes and receive the speech therapy throughout the school day for short periods of time. The specific activities worked on in the speech and language sessions should be generalized and used in the general education setting as much as possible.

Traumatic Brain Injury (TBI)

A traumatic brain injury is an acquired injury to the brain caused by an external physical force, resulting in total or partial functional disability or psychosocial impairment (or both) that may adversely affect a child's educational performance and result in the need for special education and related services. The term applies to open or closed head injuries resulting in impairments in one or more of the following areas: cognition, speech/language, memory, attention, ability to reason, abstract thinking, judgment, problem-solving, sensory, perceptual and motor abilities, psychosocial behavior, physical functions, and information processing. The term does not apply to brain injuries that are congenital or degenerative or to brain injuries induced by birth trauma.

Most traumatic brain injuries are caused by automobile, motorcycle, or bicycle accidents, falls, assaults, gunshot wounds, and child abuse. Many children who have suffered serious head injury also experience subsequent problems in learning, behavior, and adjustment. The children may also display inappropriate or exaggerated behavior ranging from extreme aggressiveness to apathetic behavior. Children may also have difficulty paying attention and retaining new information.

Educational Approaches for Traumatic Brain Injuries

Children who re-enter school will experience deficits from their injuries compounded by their extended absence from school. These students will likely require academic, psychological, and family support. Few educational programs have been specifically designed for this population; however, these children will most likely need special services in order to successfully progress in their learning.

Blind / Visually Impaired

The term blind/visually impaired means a medically verified visual impairment accompanied by a limitation in sight that interferes with acquiring information or interaction with the environment to the extent that special education and related services may be needed.

Specific criteria must be met in order to be eligible for special education services in the area of visually impaired. There must be a medically verified visual impairment accompanied by limitation in sight. Examples of these medically diagnosed visual impairments may include but are not limited to the examples listed below.

Albinism

Albinism is an inherited condition which causes decreased pigment either in the skin, hair, and eyes, or in the eyes alone. Albinism is present at birth and does not become worse over time. With corrective lenses, visual acuity usually measures around

20/100 to 20/200, although it may be as good as 20/40. Approximately 1 in 20,000 children are born with this condition.

Medical Treatment for Albinism

Albinism is most often treated with the use of tinted or pinhole contact lenses, absorptive lenses, or optical aids, although these may not always be helpful. Adjusting the lighting and conditions for individuals and having them wear sunglasses and seek shade when outdoors are essential for those who are very sensitive to bright lighting.

Cataract

A cataract is a clouding of the eye lens. Its cause could be the result of heredity, an infection, severe malnutrition, the mother's drug use during pregnancy, or trauma. Symptoms include a whitish appearance of the pupil and blurred vision.

Medical Treatment for Cataracts

The only medical treatment for cataracts is surgery. Cataracts should be removed within the first few months of life if acuity is to develop normally. Contact lenses or glasses may help with vision acuity. A child with a central cataract may have some unusual head positions, since the child is essentially "looking around" the cataract to help vision. Magnification is helpful in some cases.

Glaucoma

Glaucoma refers to a group of diseases of the eye which cause progressive damage to the optic nerve due to increased pressure within the eyeball. If glaucoma is treated before severe nerve damage results, glaucoma need not cause blindness or severe vision loss. As the optic nerve deteriorates, blind spots develop. If left untreated, the result may be total blindness. Signs and symptoms of glaucoma include blurred vision (usually in one eye), haloes appearing around lights, pain in the eye, and reddening of the eye.

Medical Treatment for Glaucoma

Glaucoma is often treated through surgery. An operation is performed which creates a drainage hole in the iris. This is done by a laser and is very quick with few repercussions.

Nystagmus

Nystagmus is an involuntary, rhythmical, repeated movement of one or both eyes. Movements may be horizontal, vertical, or circular and are often rapid and jerky. Nystagmus may accompany neurological disorders or may be caused from a reaction to certain drugs.

Medical Treatment for Nystagmus

There is no generally accepted treatment for nystagmus; however, certain types of jerky nystagmus show improvement throughout childhood. Children with nystagmus may tend to lose their place during reading instruction and may need help. Use of an index card to underline a sentence, or a typoscope (a card with a hole to view one word or line at a time) can be helpful. As children with nystagmus mature, they seem to need these support devices less often, as they tend to compensate in other ways.

Retinitis Pigmentosa (R.P.)

Retinitis Pigmentosa is a condition in which the retinas in both eyes slowly deteriorate. There is often no apparent reason for its occurrence. As the disease progresses, night vision deteriorates and peripheral vision, is lost producing "tunnel vision." This often leads to legal blindness.

Medical Treatment for Retinitis Pigmentosa

There is no known treatment for Retinitis Pigmentosa. A variety of optical aids, such as magnifiers, telescopes, and prism lenses, may be effective.

Educational Approaches for Visual Impairments

Teachers of visually impaired children need specialized skills along with knowledge and creativity. Most children who are blind learn to read using Braille. They may also learn to type and use special equipment for mathematics, social studies, and science, as well as learning to feel and read regular print while listening to it on a taped recording. Children with low vision should learn to use their residual vision as efficiently as possible. They may use optical aids and large print to read regular type. Encourage all visually impaired children to develop and utilize their listening skills.

Section II

The Special Education Process

Special Education Flow Chart

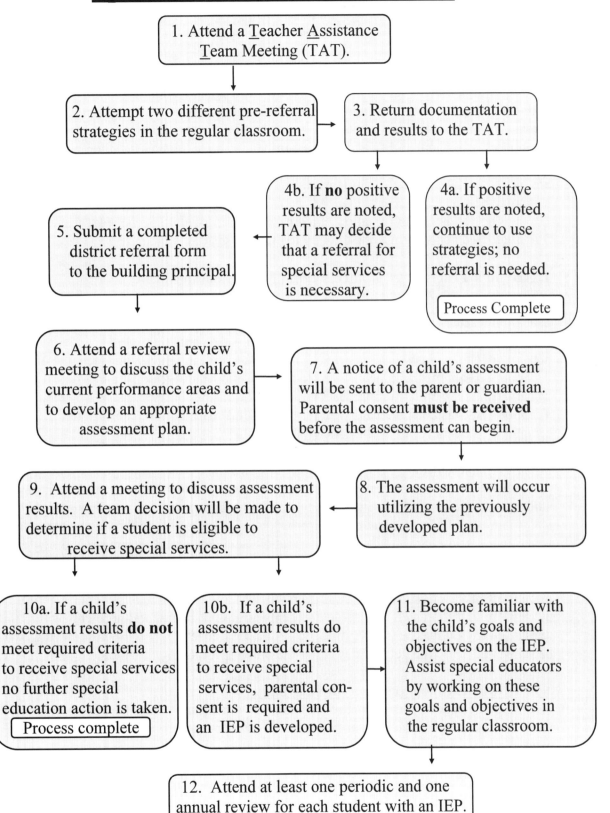

1. Attend a Teacher Assistance Team Meeting (TAT).

2. Attempt two different pre-referral strategies in the regular classroom.

3. Return documentation and results to the TAT.

4b. If **no** positive results are noted, TAT may decide that a referral for special services is necessary.

4a. If positive results are noted, continue to use strategies; no referral is needed.

Process Complete

5. Submit a completed district referral form to the building principal.

6. Attend a referral review meeting to discuss the child's current performance areas and to develop an appropriate assessment plan.

7. A notice of a child's assessment will be sent to the parent or guardian. Parental consent **must be received** before the assessment can begin.

9. Attend a meeting to discuss assessment results. A team decision will be made to determine if a student is eligible to receive special services.

8. The assessment will occur utilizing the previously developed plan.

10a. If a child's assessment results **do not** meet required criteria to receive special services no further special education action is taken.

Process complete

10b. If a child's assessment results do meet required criteria to receive special services, parental consent is required and an IEP is developed.

11. Become familiar with the child's goals and objectives on the IEP. Assist special educators by working on these goals and objectives in the regular classroom.

12. Attend at least one periodic and one annual review for each student with an IEP.

Explanation of the Process

Since education is a state function, the special education process is governed by state statutes as well as federal law. The state's special education laws must be consistent with federal laws; however, there will be differences between states. Some states have provisions that go beyond what is required by IDEA, and may provide students with disabilities additional rights and protections under state statutes. If there is a conflict between the two laws, the federal law supersedes the state law. The guidelines listed here are based on IDEA and also comparison of several state statutes. The timelines for your state may be slightly different.

The following information explains each step of the special education process. The numbered items correspond directly to the flow chart shown on page 31.

1. Attend a Teacher Assistance Team (TAT) meeting.

The Teacher Assistance Team (TAT) is a committee formed to assist regular education teachers who have concerns about a student who is struggling to learn or whose behavior is interfering with his own or affecting other students' ability to learn in the general education classroom. Depending upon the school in which you teach, the Teacher Assistance Team may also be referred to as the Child Study Team, Pre-Placement Team, or perhaps the Pre-Referral Intervention Team. For this publication, the Teacher Assistant Team or TAT has been selected. The purpose of this team is to screen the student before sending the student for a special education referral.

If you have a concern about a specific student you will need to contact a member of the TAT and schedule a time to discuss the student. At the meeting you will need to be prepared to share information related to the academic and/or behavioral difficulties the student is experiencing, discuss the type of supports you have implemented in the classroom, share information about the progress or regression seen throughout the school year, and disclose any additional information such as parental concerns or medical information that will help the TAT know the student better. After the discussion, the team will offer suggestions and provide several different intervention strategies for you to implement in the classroom. (An intervention strategy is a planned, systematic effort by the regular education staff to resolve apparent learning or behavioral problems within the regular education classroom.) At the end of the TAT meeting, a follow-up meeting will be scheduled approximately 30 days after the initial meeting.

Note to teachers about parent(s) or guardian(s)

It is important to keep the parent(s) or guardian(s) informed of their child's progress in school. If you have not discussed with them your concerns at school, you will need to contact them at this time.

2. Return to the classroom and implement at least two of the suggested strategies.

Many states require that two documented instructional strategies, alternatives, or interventions must be attempted in the general education setting before a special education referral is made. As the classroom teacher, you will be responsible to implement the strategies and provide the documentation regarding the results of the intervention strategies. The interventions should be tried for at least 30 days.

In case of an emergency situation, the documented interventions may be waived.

Note to teachers about parent(s) or guardian(s)

Notify the parent(s) or guardian(s) that you have discussed your concerns related to their child with members of the TAT. Share the results of the meeting and discuss the different intervention strategies you will be implementing in the classroom.

3. In approximately 30 days, present your documentation and the results of the interventions at a TAT meeting.

At the follow-up TAT meeting, the results of the two (or more) interventions will be reviewed and discussed. It is important to bring the following to the meeting: the intervention list, documentation of the results, and any additional information or observations that would be beneficial to the team.

Note to teachers about parent(s) or guardian(s)

Before returning to the TAT meeting, inform the child's parent(s) or guardian(s) the results of the intervention strategies. Let them know that you will be attending another meeting to discuss the results and will notify the parents of the TAT decision.

4a. If positive results are shown with the use of the intervention strategies, continue to implement the strategies in the classroom.

If improvement is noted, the TAT would probably decide that a special education referral not necessary at the present time. A follow-up meeting may be scheduled to review the student's progress at a later time.

Note to teachers about parent(s) or guardian(s)

Inform the child's parent(s) or guardian(s) that the intervention strategies has produced positive results, and that you will continue to use the strategies with their child in the classroom, and that there will be no special education referral at this time.

4b. If positive results are not apparent and /or the target behaviors are worsening, the TAT members may decide that a referral for special education services is necessary.

Note to teachers about parent(s) or guardian(s)

Inform the child's parent(s) or guardian(s) that the intervention strategies attempted did not provide positive results and therefore, the committee has decided that a referral to special education is appropriate. Explain that a "referral" is a formal and ongoing process to review information related to the student. An effective referral process will need to utilize relevant information from a full range of sources including home, school, and community. Emphasize to the parents that their involvement in this process is essential.

5. Complete the district "Referral for Special Education" form.

You will need to complete the district referral form. The results of the pre-referral intervention strategies and student-specific demographic information regarding name, age, grade, parent's name, etc., will be listed on this form. Once the form is complete, sign it and submit it to the building administrator for his or her signature as well. You will be notified when the referral review meeting will take place.

Note to teachers about parent(s) or guardian(s)

Notify the parent(s) or guardian(s) that you have completed and submitted the referral form to the administrator, and that a meeting will be held to discuss the special education referral. The parent(s) or guardian(s) have the right to be informed in advance of the date and time of this meeting. Encourage the parent(s) or guardian(s) to make every effort to attend this first meeting, as their input is important.

6. Attend a referral review meeting.

After the administrator has signed the district referral form, the school psychologist and special education staff will be informed of the referral. A special education staff member will be responsible for arranging the referral review meeting. At the meeting, the team will discuss the issues and concerns surrounding the student and will develop an assessment plan to be followed during the referral process.

The student's team will consist of the student's parent(s) or guardian(s), classroom teacher, school psychologist, principal, and one or more of the special education staff who will be involved in the assessment process. The special education staff is determined by the needs of the student. If academic concerns are the issue, a Learning Disabled teacher is involved; if behaviors are the issue, the Emotional/Behavioral Disorders teacher is involved; if speech or language is a concern, the Speech and Language teacher is involved, and so forth. If there is a combination of issues, two or more specialists will be invited to the meeting.

At the meeting, the referral review form will be completed as well as an assessment plan. The following information will be discussed and documented on the form.

Referral Review Form

Student's present level of performance. The team will discuss and review the student's performance in the following areas.

1. **Intellectual functioning:** This section refers to the student's cognitive ability or IQ.

2. **Academic performance:** This area discusses the student's academic performance in the classroom. Specific information related to the curriculum will be addressed. The general education teacher will be asked to provide information regarding the student's academic performance in the classroom.

3. **Communicative status:** This area examines the student's ability to communicate with others (age-peers, older peers, teachers, and adults) in order to get his or her needs met. Parent(s) or guardian(s) and classroom teachers will be asked to provide information in this area.

4. **Motor ability:** Discussion in this area includes both fine and gross motor skills. Fine motor skills such as handwriting and cutting will be discussed. In the area of gross motor skills, physical education activities such as running, jumping rope, and skipping may be discussed. Parent(s) or guardian(s) and classroom teachers would be asked to provide information in this area.

5. **Vocational potential:** If a student is 14 years old or entering 9th grade (during the effective dates of the IEP), this area must be addressed. Five areas of transition will be considered: jobs and job training, recreation and leisure, home-independent living, community participation, and post-secondary training and learning opportunities. The area of vocational potential will rarely be utilized for elementary students.

6. **Sensory status:** This area includes both the visual and hearing components. Any concerns regarding a student's sight or hearing abilities will be discussed. Information gathered from the student's parent(s) or guardian(s) will be essential.

7. **Physical status:** A student's overall health condition and general health will be noted in this section. Parental or guardian input will be critical for this area.

8. **Emotional and social development:** This section covers the child's interactions with peers and adults in social situation, as well as how the child is able to emotionally handle different situations and feelings.

9. **Behavior:** The student's overall behavior is noted here. Behavior concerns in the classroom, the community, or at home, are addressed in this section. Input from teacher(s) and parent(s) or guardian(s) is important for this section.

10. **Functional skills:** Functional skills include information related to how the student is able to care for him or herself and how the student independently performs daily-living skills. Issues such as toilet training, dressing, and feeding and self-care will be discussed. Other functional skills will include caring for pets, keeping personal space clean, bathing and showering, etc. Parental or guardian input will be imperative.

Note to teachers about parent(s) or guardian(s)

It is essential that the student's parent(s) or guardian(s) be involved in this initial referral review meeting. Crucial information regarding the student's communicative status, physical status, emotional and social development, behavior, functional skills, and medical information often only can be provided only by the student's parent(s) or guardian(s).

Development of the Assessment Plan

After the referral review is completed and all of the above areas have been discussed, an assessment plan will be developed. An assessment is an evaluation of a student's strengths and weaknesses by using different testing instruments. It is important for the team to use a variety of assessment tools, both formal and informal, to gather relevant, functional, and developmental information about a student. This information can be gathered in a variety of ways.

1. **Traditional assessments** are formal, standardized tools designed to test the student's level of functioning in specific areas. The assessments are used to gather in-depth information relating to a student's capabilities and performance. The results gathered during formal assessments are used to compare the student's level of performance to the performance of other students of the same age and grade level. The tests provide information that will help to determine if the student is performing above, below, or at the same level as other students of the same age and grade-level.

2. **Nontraditional assessments** are additional means to gather valuable information. These assessments are informal methods of gathering systematic information about a student's functioning in a particular setting. This may include looking at classwork samples, observations in multiple settings, student portfolios, and any additional ways to gather information and learn more about the child.

Special Education Staff Responsibility

After the team determines which assessments will be administered, the team members must decide who is responsible for administering the assessments.

Completion of the "Notice of Education Assessment/Reassessment" form

All information discussed at this meeting, including the assessment methods used and the special education staff responsibility, will be documented on the "Notice of Education Assessment/Reassessment" form.

7. Obtain parental consent prior to beginning to assess.

A copy of the "Notice of Educational Assessment/Reassessment" must be provided to the parent(s) or guardian(s) of the student. A parent or guardian must sign the form and give consent before any assessments can take place. The school **cannot** proceed with any assessment activities without this written consent.

Note to teachers about parent(s) or guardian(s)

Explain to the parent(s) or guardian(s) that they must give consent by signing of the Notice of Educational Assessment/Reassessment form. The assessment cannot begin until that form is signed and returned to the school. Giving consent to assess **does not mean** that the parent or guardian is giving consent for the child to **receive** special education services. It only means that the Special Education team is given permission to assess the child. If a parent has questions related to the assessment, you may want to suggest he or she contact the school psychologist, the administrator, or the special education teacher(s) listed on the form.

8. Complete the assessment.

Once the permission is signed and returned, the assessment period begins. The team must conduct the assessment within a reasonable amount of time. The time should not exceed 30 calendar days from the date that the school receives the signed parental permission form. When all assessments are complete, the special education team will compile the findings from the formal and informal assessments and summarize the information on the Assessment Summary Report. The report will include test results and interpretations, present level of performance in the areas assessed, and the team's judgment regarding eligibility for services. The assessment summary report must also have all team members' names and titles, and the date.

Note to teachers about parent(s) or guardian(s)

Inform the parent(s) or guardian(s) that once the assessment is complete, a meeting will be set up to discuss the results of the assessments. The parent(s) or guardian(s) must receive a written notice from the special education department about the upcoming meeting date and time. They should be notified early enough so they have adequate time to make arrangements to attend. You may want to call the parents several days before the meeting as a reminder and to be sure they understand the importance of the meeting. The results of the testing data will be presented and the special education team will make recommendations of how to proceed.

9. Attend a meeting to discuss the assessment results.

During this meeting, each team member who has assessed the student will describe the assessment procedure and discuss the results. If at any time you do not understand the terminology or the information presented, be sure to ask for clarification. If you do not understand, it is likely that the parents may not understand either. Once all assessment results have been shared, the team will determine whether the student meets the specific criteria to receive service. If a child is eligible to receive service, that conclusion must be recorded on the assessment summary report.

10a. If the child does not qualify for special services, the process is complete.

If the assessment results indicate that a child **does not** qualify to receive special education services under any one of the fourteen categories, the special education process is complete. No further special education action can be taken.

10b. If the child qualifies for special services, further action is taken.

If the assessment results indicate that the child qualifies for special education services, an Individualized Education Plan (IEP) must be written. If time permits, the IEP may be written after the assessment results have been discussed and eligibility is determined. The second option is to schedule a separate meeting within 30 calendar days. The meeting must be held at a time when the student's parent(s) or guardian(s) can attend.

When writing the IEP, all team members must be present. Required team members include the parent(s) or guardian(s), the special education teacher, the general education teacher, a representative of the school district (a special education administrator, or school administrator), and any additional people at parental or district discretion.

Notes to teachers about parent(s) of guardian(s)

Encourage parent(s) or guardian(s) to ask any questions that they may have. You want to be sure they understand the information discussed and the plan developed for their child. Be aware that the parents have received a large amount of information. Often, once the information is reread at home, questions will arise.

Explanation of the Individualized Education Plan (IEP)

Purpose. An Individualized Education Plan, or IEP, is the result of a process to ensure that individuals with disabilities receive appropriate educational planning to accommodate their unique instructional needs and that these needs are met in an appropriate learning environment. An IEP is a written legal document that is developed, reviewed, and revised as needed. The IEP is reviewed annually and the student must be reassessed every three years.

Writing the IEP. The IEP must include specific components to ensure that all areas of the student's education will be met. The first component of the IEP is to make a statement which describes the student's present levels of educational performance in the following areas:

Component A:
1) intellectual functioning
2) academic performance
3) communicative status
4) motor ability
5) vocational potential
6) sensory status
7) physical status
8) emotional and social development
9) behavior
10) functional skills

Component B: After discussing the student's present level of performance in the ten areas listed above, the team must decide which specific, student-based instructional needs must be addressed.

Component C: At least one annual goal must be written for each of the needs identified by the IEP team. For each goal, short-term objectives must be written as well.

> **Goals:** The annual goals in the IEP are statements that describe what a child with a disability can reasonably be expected to accomplish within a twelve-month period. There should be a direct relationship between annual goals and the student's instructional needs.

> **Objectives:** Short-term objectives are measurable, intermediate steps between the present level of performance of a student and the annual goals that are established. The objectives are developed based on a logical breakdown of the major components of the annual goal, and can serve as milestones for measuring progress toward meeting the goals.

> **Progress reviews:** The IEP team must discuss a plan for reviewing the progress of the goals and objectives. There must be at least **one periodic** and **one annual review.** The purpose of the review is to assess the student's progress in relation to the goals and objectives and to update the IEP if necessary.

Component D: The IEP must include a statement of the specific special education and related services to be provided to the student. The IEP must list the person responsible for providing the service, the total minutes of service per week, and the date that the service will begin.

Component E: The team must write a statement of justification which states how the team ensures that the proposed plan is going to provide for the least restrictive environment for the student. The statement should include opportunities to participate and progress in the general education curriculum and school activities, as well as state any modifications and adaptations the student may need in order to be successful.

Modification and adaptations are ways in which the regular education curriculum or classroom environment is changed for a student with special needs in order to assist the student in being more successful in the classroom. Examples of specific adaptations or modifications are provided in Section III.

The IEP must be written and agreed upon by all team members.

Note to teachers about parent(s) or guardian(s)

Before a student's special education services can begin for the first time, the student's parent(s) or guardian(s) must give written consent, agreeing to the IEP and the proposed plan.

11. Know the goals and objectives on the IEP.

A classroom teacher must be familiar with a student's IEP contents, especially the goals, objectives, and modifications which must be implemented in the general education classroom.

12. Attend a periodic and annual review of the IEP.

The student's progress toward the IEP goals and objectives must be reviewed at least two times during the year. A **periodic review** is scheduled at least one time (more frequent if needed) during the year to discuss a student's progress. The periodic review is most often held during a parent-teacher conference. An **annual review** must be completed within one year of the date on the IEP. At the annual review, the IEP is reviewed, revised, and rewritten. If the student has met some or all of the goals and objectives on the IEP, new goals and objectives must be written to address the current educational performance issues. It is at the IEP annual review that the team also determines whether or not the student continues to need special education services.

Note to teachers about parent(s) or guardian(s)

Encourage the parent(s) or guardian(s) to attend both the periodic review and annual reviews, as their input is essential. Parent(s) or guardian(s) do have the right to request an IEP meeting at any time if they feel one is necessary. For example, if the parent(s) or guardian(s) believe their child is not progressing satisfactorily or there is a problem with the current IEP, it would be appropriate for the parent to request an IEP meeting.

A student who receives special education services must be reassessed every 3 years to ensure that the student continues to meet the eligibility criteria and continues to require special education services.

Traditional Formal Assessments

This section includes an overview of some of the most common assessment tools used. Some assessment tools must be administered by the school psychologist whereas others are administered by a special education teacher. The person who administrates the test is also responsible for interpreting the assessment and sharing the results with the IEP team.

Specific terminology is used when reporting assessment results. Listed below, in alphabetical order, are the most common terms used. It is important to be familiar with these terms before attending the IEP assessment summary meeting.

Explanation of Test Scores

Age Equivalents

An age equivalent score is a very general score used to compare the performance of children at the same age with one another. These scores express test performance in terms of the familiar units of chronological age. For example, if a student receives an age score of 7.6 (7 years, 6 months) on a test it means the student has performed as well as the average 7-year 6-month-old child.

Grade Equivalents

A grade-equivalent score is a general score used to compare the performance of children in the same grade with one another. The scores express test performance in terms of grade levels. For example, a student who receives a score of 4.5 is performing as well as the average student in the 4th grade – 5th month.

Percentile Ranks

Percentile ranks represent the percentage of individuals within the norm group who achieved this raw score or a lower one. If a student earns a percentile rank of 62, it can be said that the student performed at a level equal to or greater than 62% of the norm group, and at a level lower than that of the remaining 28% of the norm group.

Raw Scores

The first step in scoring a test is to determine the raw score. The raw score normally indicates the number of items correctly answered on a test.

Scaled Scores

Scaled scores most frequently refer to subtest scores. Most often, scaled scores place the average score at 10, thus if a student receives a scaled score of 10, the student is performing in the average range when compared to the norm group of the same age.

Students who receive a scaled score of 19 would fall in the above-average range whereas students who receive a scaled score of 3 fall in the below-average range.

17 and above	**Above Average**
14 to 16	**High Average**
7 to 13	**AVERAGE**
4 to 6	**Low Average**
3 and below	**Below Average**

Standard Scores

Standard scores are often used to report overall test performance and are useful for comparing several different test scores for the same student. Standard scores transform the "raw" score to fit a normal curve. Normally, standard scores have a mean of 100 and a standard deviation of 15. This means that if a student received a standard score of 100 the student's score could range between 85 and 115. This score would fall in the average range.

130 and above	**Above Average**
116 to 129	**High Average**
85 to 115	**AVERAGE**
71 to 84	**Low Average**
70 and below	**Below Average**

Intellectual Functioning Assessments

Wechsler Intelligence Scales for Children- (WISC-IV)

This is a standardized test that is administered individually to children ages 6.0 to 17.0. It assesses general intellectual functioning. The results of this battery of tests will also provide information regarding the student's strengths and weaknesses in specific areas of ability. The test has 15 subtests, but only 10 subtests are required to be administered in order to determine IQ scores. The test is divided into four main sections: the *verbal index* which consists of five subtests, the *perceptual reasoning index* which consists of 5 subtests, the *working memory index* and the *processing speed index*, each consisting of 3 subtests.

When determining results of the WISC-IV, four composite scores are given. The Full Scale IQ is based on the performance of all combined scales.

The global IQ scores are just like **Standard Scores** and can be interpreted using the Standard Score criteria. Four factor-based Index Scores are also produced by combining various subtests. These Index Scores are the same as Standard Scores as well and can be interpreted using the Standard Score criteria. Individual subtest **Scaled Scores** are also provided.

Wechsler Preschool and Primary Scale of Intelligence-Third Edition (WPPSI-III)

This is a test administered individually to children ages 2.6 to 7.3 years old. The results of this battery of tests will provide information regarding the student's strengths and weaknesses in specific areas of ability. There are four core subtests and one supplemental Verbal subtest for children aged 2.6-3.11. For children aged 4.0-7.3 there are seven core subtests with two Verbal and Performance supplemental subtests. The test takes approximately 35 minutes for younger children and 50 minutes for older children. Results from subtests given are used to provide information regarding a child's verbal and non-verbal fluid reasoning, receptive versus expressive vocabulary, and processing speed.

When determining results of the WPPSI-III, age specific scaled scores and IQ scores are provided. The global IQ scores can be interpreted using the **Standard Score** criteria. Individual subtest **Scaled Scores** are also provided.

Woodcock-Johnson Psycho-Educational Battery III-Test of Cognitive Ability (Part 1)

The Woodcock-Johnson test has two parts. The first part measures a student's cognitive ability and the second part measures the student's school performance or achievement. Part One of this test is used to determine a student's intellectual ability. This test is administered individually and usually takes less than one hour to administer the entire standard battery. The test can be used for individuals, ages 2.0 to 90+ years old and has scoring norms for grades K-12 and college (undergraduate and graduate level).

There are seven subtests that make up the Standard Battery and 14 supplemental subtests comprise the Extended Battery. The entire Standard Battery must be administered and then if further information is desired, the Extended Battery may be administered. Depending on the purpose and extent of the assessment, one, several or all of the Extended Battery tests may be administered. This battery is difficult to administer and should be administered by the school psychologist.

Many results are produced by this assessment battery. The Broad Ability Scale summarizes the student's performance on the standard battery. A Broad Ability Extended Scale takes into account all of the standard battery subtests as well as seven of the supplementary subtests. Results can also be reported by subtest, cognitive factor, and areas of scholastic aptitude. More than 35 subtest and area results are produced and each result can be expressed as an **Age-Equivalent, Grade-Equivalent, Standard Score,** and **Percentile Rank.**

Stanford-Binet Intelligence Scale: Fifth Edition (SB5)

The Stanford-Binet Intelligence Scale: Fifth Edition is considered to be a standard tool of many school psychologists. This test, unlike the Wechsler version provides multiple IQ scores instead of one single IQ score. This test offers a comprehensive measurement of five factors including fluid reasoning, knowledge, quantitative reasoning, visual-spatial processing, and working memory.

The SB5 is appropriate to be used as an initial vocabulary test which, along with the student's age, determines the number and level of subtests to be administered. The total testing time ranges from 45-90 minutes. Raw scores are based on the number of items answered and converted into a standard age score, similar to an IQ measure. The testing results can be expressed as an **Age-Equivalent** and **Scaled Score**.

Adaptive Behavior Measures

Adaptive behavior is related to both personal independence and social responsibility. Expected adaptive behavior varies with the age of the individual. Preschool children are expected to learn to walk, talk, and interact with family members. School-aged children are expected to widen their circle of acquaintances and add academic skills to their repertoire. A student's adaptive behavior is assessed when a student is suspected of being mild-moderate or moderate-severely mentally impaired or of having Autistic characteristics.

Adaptive behavior is usually not measured directly. Instead the student's parents or teachers are used as informants about the student's current nonacademic functioning. The parents are usually interviewed and the teachers often complete written questionnaires.

AAMR Adaptive Behavior Scale - School (2nd Ed.) (ABS-S:2)

The ABS-S:2 is an indirect measure of adaptive and maladaptive behavior. This test can be used with children and young adults ages 3.0 to 21.0 with mental impairments. It may also be used with children and teenagers without mental impairments between the ages 3.0- to 18.0 years. Results of the ABS-S:2 can be used to identify strengths and weaknesses in adaptive behavior, can determine if a student shows below-average performance, and can document student progress. ABS-S:2 is a questionnaire and can be completed by professionals such as teachers. If the professional is unable to make judgments regarding the student's skill levels, the scale may be administered by a trained professional in an interview format with a parent or other adult who knows the student well. Part One of the ABS-S:2 addresses adaptive behavior skills related to personal independence; Part Two is concerned with social behaviors. The assessment includes sixteen domains. The sixteen domains are separated into "Five Factors." The Five Factors are: Personal Self-Sufficiency, Community Self-Sufficiency, Personal-Social Responsibility, Social Adjustment, and Personal Adjustment.

Results of the ABS-S:2 are reported using **Percentile Ranks** and **Scaled Scores** for each of the 16 domains as well as for the Five Factor scores. A Quotient or overall test score can also be explained using **Percentile Ranks** and **Standard Scores. Age-Equivalent Scores** can be obtained for Part One Factors (Factors 1, 2 and 3) only.

Vineland Adaptive Behavior Scales, Second Edition (Vineland-II)

The Vineland Adaptive Behavior Scales, Second Edition provides a measure of personal and social skills from birth to adulthood. The assessment contains four separate scales: two interview editions (a survey from and an expanded form), a parent/caregiver rating form, and a teacher rating form. The interview editions are used by trained interviewers with parents or others who know the student well. The survey form includes fewer items than the expanded interview form and consequently requires less administration time. The Vineland-II has an expanded age range encompassing birth to age 90 when using the Survey Interview, Expanded Interview and the Parent/Caregiver Rating Forms and ages 3 to 21.11 using the Teacher Rating Form.

Use of the Vineland-II aids in diagnosing and classifying mental retardation and other disorders, such as Autism, Asperger Syndrome, and developmental delays. The content and scales of the Vineland-II are organized within a four domain structure; Communication; Daily Living; Socialization and Motor Skills as well as an optional Maladaptive Behavior Index which provides more in-depth information.

Standard Scores are used to report results of the Vineland-II. These Standard Scores are available for each of the four adaptive behavior domains as well as for the total test or Composite score summarizing the domains.

Academic Achievement Assessments

These assessments measure a student's academic level in reading, mathematics, written language, social studies, and science. Results of these tests are used to determine a student's achievement of school skills as compared to other age- or grade-level peers.

Woodcock-Johnson Psycho-Educational Battery III - Revised Tests of Achievement (Part 2)

The Tests of Achievement is the 2nd part of the two-part Woodcock Johnson Psycho-Educational Battery, Revised. The first part assesses a student's cognitive ability, and is described in the Cognitive Assessments section. Part 2 of this assessment is designed to assess and provide information about four areas of the curriculum: reading, mathematics, written language, and knowledge (social studies, science, and humanities). The standard battery contains 9 subtests, and the supplemental battery contains 5 additional subtests.

This achievement assessment can adequately assess skills in people ages 2 to 90+, and in grades K-12 and college age. This assessment is easy to administer and is designed for use by professionals such as special education teachers who are trained in the administration and interpretation of individual tests. The test is administered using an easel-style notebook. The test administrator uses a test protocol to record student's answers.

Results produced by the Woodcock Johnson Test of Achievement can be reported by subtests, academic areas, and subskills. More than 30 subtest and academic area results are produced, and each result can be expressed in a variety of scores including **Age-Equivalents, Grade-Equivalents, Standard Scores** and **Percentile Ranks.**

Wechsler Individual Achievement Test, Second Edition (WIAT-II)

This academic achievement test is the only achievement battery empirically linked with the Wechsler Intelligence Scale for children- Fourth Edition (WISC-IV), the Wechsler Preschool and Primary Scale of Intelligence-Third Edition (WPPSI-III), and the Wechsler Adult Intelligence Scale-Third Edition (WAIS-III). The WIAT-II provides a rich source of information about an individual's academic skills and problem-solving abilities that can be used to guide appropriate intervention. It is a comprehensive yet flexible measurement tool useful for achievement skills assessment, learning disability diagnosis, special education placement, curriculum planning, and clinical appraisal of children adolescents, college students, and adults, ages 4-85.

The WIAT-II contains nine subtests. Three subtests assess reading (Pseudoword Decoding, Word Reading and Reading Comprehension), two assess math (Numerical Operations and Mathematics Reasoning), two assess written language (Spelling and Written Expression), and two assess oral language (Listening Comprehension and Oral Language). The WIAT-II does assess all the achievement areas that are included in the federal definition of a learning disability. Results of this assessment can be easily compared with the results from one of the Wechsler Individual Ability tests to see if a significant discrepancy exists between the student's ability and achievement scores. The WIAT-II does not assess science, social studies or other content subjects; however, it does provide information about oral language, which is rarely assessed by other individual achievement tests.

The WIAT-II is most often administered by a school psychologist, as the manual recommends that only professionals with graduate-level training in the use of individually administered assessment instruments are qualified to administer and interpret the test results. The results of the WIAT are best used to identify curriculum areas where a student is performing significantly below his or her age or grade peers.

Results are provided using **Standard Scores, Percentile Ranks, Age-Equivalent,** and **Grade-Equivalent** scores for all subtests administered. These same scores are also provided for the 5 composite scores given (Reading, Mathematics, Language, Writing and Total). The Total Composite score reflects all eight subtests combined.

Kaufmann Test of Educational Achievement, Second Edition (KTEA-II)

The KTEA-II is an individually administered battery that provides a flexible, thorough assessment of the key academic skills in reading, math, written language, and oral language.

There are two forms of the KTEA-II, a Brief Form and a Comprehensive Form. The Brief Form can be utilized for anyone aged 4.6 to 90 years old and provides subtests in the areas of reading, math and written language. It takes approximately 20-30 minutes to administer.

The Comprehensive Form can be administered to anyone between the ages of 4.6-25 years old and assesses the areas of reading, math and written and oral language. The administration times vary depending upon the age of the student. Approximate times are 30 minutes (PreK-K), 30 minutes (Grades 1-2), and 80 minutes (Grades 3+).

Results produced from the K-TEA include **Grade-Equivalent Scores, Standard Scores,** and **Percentile Rank** for each subtest as well as for the total test score. For each subtest given and for the Total Reading Cluster, **Grade-Equivalent** and **Age-Equivalent** scores are provided as well as **Percentile Ranks** and **Standard Scores.**

Peabody Individual Achievement Test – Revised (PIAT-R/NU)

The PIAT-R/NU is an individually administered measure of academic achievement. This revised edition includes normative updates (NU). The test is designed to provide a wide range of screening measures in six content areas. The test may be administered to students ages 5.0 to 22.11 and in kindergarten through 12th grade. The six content areas assessed by the PIAT-R/NU are as follows. The *mathematics* measures knowledge and application of mathematical concepts and facts. The *reading recognition* measures the initial prereading items, the ability to recognize the sounds associated with letters, and, in later items, oral reading of words. The *reading comprehension* section measures the student's understanding of what is read. The initial items in the *spelling* section measure the student's ability to recognize letters from their names or sounds and then measure the student's recognition of standard spellings. The *general information* section measures general encyclopedic knowledge. The final *written expression* is divided into two levels and measures story-writing skills. The total battery can be administered in approximately 30 to 40 minutes. Six individual domain scores are produced from each of the content areas as well as a Total Reading Composite, Written Language Composite, and a Total Test Score. All subtest domain scores as well as the Total Reading and Total Test Composites can be reported using **Grade-Equivalent** and **Age-Equivalent Scores**, **Percentile Ranks,** and **Standard Scores**.

Math Assessments

KeyMath Revised/NU

The KeyMath Revised/NU is an individually administered test designed to provide a comprehensive assessment of a student's understanding and application of important mathematical concepts and skills. This assessment is appropriate for students aged 5.0 - 22.0 years old and for students in grades K-12. The test consists of 13 subtests that are organized into three major areas of mathematics: Basic Concepts (foundation knowledge), Operations (computational skills), and Applications in Mathematics (the use of knowledge and computational skills).

The results from the KeyMath-R/NU help evaluators determine the student's current achievement in basic mathematics concepts, computational operations, and applications such as problem solving, estimation, time, money, and measurement. The KeyMath-R/NU is most useful as a screening device to identify possible mathematical strengths and weaknesses. The KeyMath-R/NU requires no special training to be administered. The manual states that the test can be administered by general and special education teachers, classroom aides, and other paraprofessionals, as long as the manual is followed. Test result interpretation, however, is best accomplished by professionals with some formal training in interpreting test results.

For each subtest given, results are expressed using both **Percentile Ranks** and **Scaled Scores**. **Grade-Equivalent** and **Age-Equivalent** scores, **Percentile Ranks,** and **Standard Scores** are given for the overall total test as well as for the three major areas assessed (Basic Concepts, Operations, and Applications).

Test of Mathematical Abilities (TOMA-2)

The TOMA-2 attempts to assess the attitudes a student might have toward mathematics, the understanding of the vocabulary used in a mathematical sense, and the understanding of how information related to mathematics is used. This test will effectively assess students age 8.0 to 18.11 years and requires 60-90 minutes to administer. The TOMA-2 contains five subtests: Attitude toward Math, Vocabulary, Computation, General Information, and Story Problems.

No special training is required to administer the TOMA-2; however, administrators should study the manual prior to administering the TOMA-2 for the first time. The results of the test may be reported in **Standard Scores, Percentile Ranks, Grade-Equivalent Scores,** or **Age-Equivalent Scores.** The standard scores of the core battery are combined to comprise a total score called the Math Quotient.

Reading Assessments

Woodcock Reading Mastery Tests-Revised (WRMT-R/NU)

The WRMT-R/NU is used to pinpoint students' strengths and weaknesses in the area of reading. There are two forms of the WRMT-R/NU: Form G and Form H. Form G is a complete battery made up of four tests of reading achievement and a readiness section; Form H is a condensed form which contains only alternate forms of the reading achievement tests.

The four subtests common to both forms are as follows: *Word Identification* in which students are shown individual words and must pronounce each word; *Word Attack* in which students are asked to pronounce nonsense words and syllables; *Word Comprehension*, in which students are asked to identify antonyms, synonyms and analogies; and *Passage Comprehension*, in which students are shown a brief passage with one word omitted and then is asked to supply the missing word. Form G contains all of the previously mentioned measures as well as three measures of reading readiness which include *Visual-Auditory Learning, Letter Identification,* and *Supplementary Letter Checklist.*

The WRMT-R/NU is designed for students from kindergarten through college and ages 5.0 through 75+, but young children and non-readers may experience success only on the readiness subtests. Each cluster of tests should take between 10-30 minutes to administer.

There is no formal training required to administer the WRMT-R/NU, although prior to administering this test for the first time, examiners should study the test manual, administer at least two practice tests, and be observed and evaluated by an experienced examiner.

The results received from the WRMT-R/NU help determine the student's current levels of achievement in reading readiness, basic reading skills, and comprehension. These results are most useful for identifying areas of strength and educational need.

The WRMT-R/NU offers a variety of scores. For each subtest given and for the Total Reading Cluster, **Grade-Equivalent** and **Age-Equivalent Scores** are provided, as are **Percentile Ranks** and **Standard Scores.**

Test of Reading Comprehension (TORC-3)

The TORC-3 does not attempt to measure all aspects of the reading process. Instead, it emphasizes comprehension skills, silent reading, and knowledge of word meanings.

The TORC-3 contains eight subtests. It is not necessary to administer all eight subtests, however, to receive an index of general reading comprehension ability. The General Comprehension Core consists of the following four subtests: *General Vocabulary*, in which students are presented with three words that are related and then given four additional words from which to choose which word best relates to the other to the first three words; *Syntactic Similarities*, in which students read five sentences and select the two that are most similar in meaning; *Paragraph Reading*, in which students read six one- or two-paragraph selections and then answer five multiple-choice questions about each; and *Sentence Sequencing,* in which five sentences that make up a paragraph are listed in random order for the student to determine the sequence in which the sentences should appear.

The Diagnostic Supplements include four of the eight subtests and can be administered if additional information is needed. The four Diagnostic Supplements include Mathematics Vocabulary, Social Studies Vocabulary, Science Vocabulary, and Reading the Directions of Schoolwork.

The TORC-3 is designed for students ages 7.0 to 17.11. Students must be able to work independently and read silently. The assessment time is approximately 30 minutes for each subtest. Administration of the TORC-3 requires no special training and is quite easy to administer. Prior to administering the TORC-3 for the first time, the administrator should give at least 3 practice tests.

Results of the TORC-3 are reported with subtest **Scaled Scores** and then an overall **Reading Comprehension Quotient (Standard Score)** which is indicative of the student's overall skills level in reading comprehension. **Percentile Ranks** are also given for each individual subtest.

Test of Word Reading Efficiency (TOWE)

The Test of Word Reading Efficiency (TOWE) is a measure of word reading accuracy and fluency. It can be administered in 5-10 minutes and provides an efficient means of monitoring the growth of two kinds of work reading skills that are critical: the ability to accurately recognize familiar words as whole units and the ability to sound out words quickly.

The TOWE contains two subtests: the Sight Word Efficiency (SWE) subtest and the Phonetic Decoding Efficiency (PDE) subtest. The SWE assesses the number of real printed words that can be accurately identified within 45 seconds. The PDE assesses the number of pronounceable printed nonsense words that can be accurately decoded within 45 seconds. Each subtest has two forms (Forms A and B) that are of equivalent difficulty, and either one or both forms of each subtest maybe given depending upon the purposes of the assessment.

Results of the TOWE are reported through **percentiles**, **standard scores**, and **age-equivalent** and **grade-equivalent scores**. **Standard Scores** are provided for each subtest as well.

Test of Early Reading Ability Complete (TERA-3)

The TERA-3 is an individually administered assessment for children ages 3.6 to 8.6 years. The entire test can be administered in 15-30 minutes. The TERA-3 assesses a child's mastery of early developing reading skills. The three subtests provided include *Alphabet,* which measures the child's knowledge of the alphabet and its uses; *Conventions*, which measures the child's knowledge of the conventions of print; and *Meaning*, which measures the construction of meaning from print. **Standard Scores** are provided for each subtest. An overall Reading Quotient is computed using all three subtest scores.

The TERA-3 results can be used to identify children who are significantly different from their peers in the early development of reading. Results from this assessment indicate children who are having reading problems and also identify children who are performing significantly above their peers.

Written Language Assessments

Test of Written Language-Third Edition (TOWL-3)

The TOWL-3 is designed to identify students who perform significantly below their peers in written expression; it will help to determine a student's strengths and weaknesses in writing. It is also used to provide directions for further educational assistance. The TOWL-3 is a completely revised edition used to document the presence of deficits in the written language area of literacy.

The test has two assessment forms. Each form assesses three components of language: the rules for punctuation, capitalization, and spelling; the use of written grammar and vocabulary; and the conceptual component, which suggests the ability to produce written products that are logical, coherent, and sequenced. When administering this test, writing is elicited by means of contrived and spontaneous formats. Spontaneous formats are assessed when students are asked to produced writing samples.

The eight subtests of the TOWL-3 measure a student's writing competence through both essay-analysis (spontaneous) formats and traditional test (contrived) formats. This assessment requires the student to have reading and writing skills. During several subtests, the student must be able to read words or sentences that prompt the writing task. This test can be administered individually or in a group setting. It is appropriate for students between the ages of 7.6 and 17.11 years. It takes approximately 90 minutes to administer the complete assessment.

Result for each subtest on the TOWL-3 can be reported through **Percentile Ranks** and **Scaled Scores.** Three global scores, (Contrived Writing Quotient, Spontaneous Writing Quotient, and Overall Written Language Quotient) are reported using **Percentile Ranks** and **Standard Scores.**

Test of Early Written Language – Second Edition (TEWL-2)

The TEWL-2 is an individual assessment instrument for children aged 3.0 to 10.11 years. The assessment has two forms, A and B. Each form includes a Basic Writing and a Contextual Writing subtest. The *Basic Writing Quotient* is a measure of a student's ability in the area of spelling, capitalization, punctuation, sentence construction, and metacognitive knowledge. Forms A and B, each consist of 57 items. The *Contextual Writing Quotient* measures the student's ability to construct a story when provided with a picture prompt. This subtest measures areas such as story format, cohesion, thematic maturity, ideation, and story structure. Each form consists of 14 items.

A Global Writing Quotient is formed by combining the standard scores from each subtest. The global writing quotient is the best indicator of a child's general writing ability.

The TEWL-2 provides Standard Score Quotients, Percentile Ranks, and Age Equivalents. It allows items to be profiled for diagnosis of strengths and weaknesses and provides direction for instructional assistance.

Oral Language Assessments

Test of Language Development - 3, Primary (TOLD-P:3 Primary) Test of Language Development - 3, Intermediate (TOLD-I:3, Intermediate)

The TOLD-3 Primary and Intermediate versions are individually administered tests used to assess oral language. The primary version is used for preschool and early elementary grade children ages 4.0 to 8.11 years. The Intermediate version is used for older elementary grade students ages 8.6 to 12.11 years. The TOLD-P:3, Primary consists of seven subtests which assess receptive and expressive phonology, syntax, and semantics skills. TOLD-I:3, Intermediate consists of six subtests which assess receptive and expressive syntax, and semantics skills. The purpose of both versions of the TOLD-3 is to identify a student's strengths and weaknesses in oral language development.

In oral language, speech is the expressive component of language, whereas listening skills are the receptive components. *Phonology* focuses on combining the features of sound into significant speech sounds (phonemes). *Syntax* is the ability to form combinations of words into acceptable phrases, clauses, and sentences. *Semantics* is the understanding and ability to make sense of the meaning of the words in sentences.

Administration of the TOLD-3 Primary and Intermediate tests is quite easy. Not all subtests are required to be administered in order to get scores.

For the TOLD-P:3, Primary, **Percentile Ranks** and **Scaled Scores** are available for each of the seven subtests. **Standard Scores** are also provided for six composite areas. The Spoken Language Quotient is a summary of performance on all subtests. The other composite areas are: Listening Quotient, Speaking Quotient and quotients for Semantics, Syntax and Phonology.

For the TOLD-I:3, Intermediate, **Percentile Ranks** and **Scaled Scores** are available for the six subtests. **Standard Scores** are also provided for five composite areas. The Spoken Language Quotient is a summary of the performance on all subtests. The other composite areas for this assessment are Listening Quotient, Speaking Quotient, Semantics Quotient, and Syntax Quotient.

Clinical Evaluation of Language Fundamentals-Third Ed. (CELF-3)

The CELF-3 is a diagnostic test which contains 11 subtests that assess syntax, semantics, and memory. This assessment is designed for students ages 5.0 to 16.11 years. The battery provides several measures of receptive and expressive syntax (forming sentences in appropriate order) and semantics (understanding what the words are telling).

Results of the CELF-3 can be provided using individual subtest **Scaled Scores** and three global **Standard Scores.** The three standard scores are given in the areas of Receptive Language, Expressive Language, and Total Language. An **Age-Equivalent** score is available for the Total Language global score.

Boehm Test of Basic Concepts-Third Edition (Boehm-3).

The Boehm-3 is an individually administered assessment for children ages 3.0 to 5.11 and is designed to evaluate young childrens' understanding fo the basic relational concepts important for language and cognitive development, as well as for later success in school. The results of the Boehm-3 can be used to identify students with weaknesses in receptive vocabulary and to identify basic concepts that students have not yet mastered. With this assessment, the students respond to a total of 50 test items. The test can be administered to an individual or a group of students.

Results of the Boehm-3 are reported as **Raw Scores**, **Percentages**, **Performance Range,** and **Percentile Rank.** .

Peabody Picture Vocabulary Test-Third Edition (PPVT-III)

The PPVT-III is an individually administered test of receptive vocabulary designed for ages 2.6 to 40.0 years. The administration of this test only requires 10 to 20 minutes. In this test, a student is shown a page containing four drawings. The administrator reads a word and the student points to or says the number of the drawing that represents the word. The PPVT-III is quick and easy to administer. This can be used as both a test of achievement (because it assesses the acquisition of English vocabulary) and as an aptitude test (because it assesses verbal skills).

The PPVT-III is not divided into subtests and only one result is obtained, a total test performance index. This total can be reported using several types of scores. **Standard Scores** are used, as are **Percentile Ranks** and **Age-Equivalent Scores.**

Behavioral Assessments

A wide variety of rating scales and checklists are available for assessing student's behavior in school, at home, and in the community.

Behavior Rating Profile - Second Edition (BRP-2)

The BRP-2 attempts to provide a comprehensive overview of a student's current behavioral status. It is appropriate for students between the ages of 6.6 and 18.6 years or for students in grades 1-12. Information for this assessment can be gathered from four types of informants: the student, teachers, parents, and peers. The student's behavior at home and in school and the student's interpersonal relationships can be assessed.

The BRP-2 consists of four profiles. The Student Rating Scale which is a self-rating scale for the student to complete, a Teacher Rating Scale which is completed by a classroom teacher who knows the student well enough to provide accurate information, the Parent Rating Scale which is completed by a parent who can provide accurate information regarding the student in the home environment, and, finally, a Peer Scale which is a sociometric technique used for the student's classmates. The purpose of the BRP-2 is to identify students with possible behavior disorders who may be in need of further assessment.

Results of the BRP-2 are described using **Scaled Scores** and **Percentile Ranks.** Several scores are available, depending on the scales administered. If the student completed the student rating scale, three separate scores are reported: Home, School, and Peer scores. There is one score for each teacher and each parent who rated the student, and each sociometric question answered by the student's peers also produces a score.

Behavior Evaluation Scale-2 (BES-2).

The BES-2 is designed to identify strengths and weaknesses in five behavioral domains of students in grades K-12. There are 76 behavior descriptions which the informant must rate according to frequency of those behaviors occurring. There are seven frequency rating choices, ranging from "never or not observed" to "continuously throughout the day." The 76 specific behaviors are divided into the five types of behavior disorders: Learning Problems, Interpersonal Difficulties, Inappropriate Behavior, Unhappiness/Depression, and Physical Symptoms/Fears.

It is recommended that teachers observe students for at least one month before completing the rating scale. The informant should be the teacher who has the primary instructional responsibility and the most contact with the student to ensure that precise completion is occurring.

Subscale **Scaled Scores** and **Percentile Ranks** are distributed for the five behavior disorder areas named above. **Standard Scores** and **Percentile Ranks** are used to describe the Overall Behavior Quotient which combines all five subscales for a total behavior score.

Attention Deficit Disorders Evaluation Scale (ADDES-3)
(Home Version and School Version)

The ADDES-3 is a rating scale designed for use with school-aged children, and adolescents, ages 4.0 to 18.0 years old. Both a school and home version are available and it asks about specific behaviors which reflect inattention, impulsivity, and hyperactivity. The School Version can be completed in approximately 15 minutes and includes 60 items easily observed and documented by educational personnel. The Home Version can be completed by a parent or guardian in approximately 12 minutes and includes 46 items representing behaviors exhibited in and around the home environment. The informant is asked to rate each specific behavior according to the frequency with which it occurs. The *Likert Scale* consists of a range of five behavior ratings.

Two types of results are produced by the ADDES-3. There are three subscales (Inattentive, Impulsive, and Hyperactive) which receive separate **Scaled Scores**. The overall total scale, which combines the three subscales, is described by a **Percentile Rank.**

Self Esteem Index (SEI)

The SEI is a self-report rating scale for students ages 8.0-18.11 years. It can be administered individually or as a group assessment. The index contains 80 statements that students rate on a Likert Scale rating. The ratings are always true, usually true, usually false, or always false. Each statement fits into one of the following four self-esteem scales: perception of familial acceptance, perception of academic competence, perception of peer popularity, and perception of personal security.

Results of the SEI are described through **Scaled Scores** and **Percentile Ranks** for the four self-esteem scales. Scores on the four scales are combined to produce a total test Self-Esteem Quotient. This quotient is provided through a **Percentile Rank** and a **Standard Score.**

Conners' Teacher Rating Scale (CTRS) and Conners' Parent Rating Scale (CPRS)

The Conners' Rating Scales (both the teacher and parent scales) are measures that can be used for assessing attention-deficit/hyperactivity disorder (ADHD) in children and adolescents. This rating scale can be used to rate the behavior of children ages 3.0 to 17.0 years. Included are long and short forms for both the teacher and parent versions. Results are reported with both **Scaled Scores** and **Percentile Ranks** for the scales.

Nontraditional Forms of Assessment

The previous assessments will be administered by the special education team. As the classroom teacher, you have a wealth of information about the student. The following information can be compiled and then compared to the assessment data. These non-standardized forms of assessment are very helpful when determining the IEP goals and objectives as they are tied directly to the classroom curriculum.

1. **Information assessment:** Information gathered through the Teacher's Assistance Team (TAT) or other pre-referral activities should be helpful.

2. **Environmental assessment:** Observe the student in various learning environments and settings where the student routinely operates to determine how the environment may affect the student's performance.

3. **Portfolio assessment:** Collect and analyze work samples from the student including classroom-based assessments, daily work, homework assignments and projects.

4. **Curriculum-based assessment:** This is a direct evaluation tied to the curriculum content. For example, reading rate and fluency information may be gathered by asking the student to read aloud from the basal reader. Classroom math assessments may be analyzed for errors. The information is compiled and the student's performance is compared to the performance of his peer group.

5. **Diagnostic teaching assessment:** Implement the results from diagnostic teaching methods or other systematic methods of instruction.

6. **Learning-style inventory:** Assess the student's learning style to determine how the student learns and solves problems.

7. **Information gathering:** Interview persons who can provide key information (e.g., student, parent, previous teachers).

Special Education Acronyms and Abbreviations

ADD	Attention Deficit Disorder
ADHD	Attention Deficit Hyperactivity Disorder
BD	Behavior Disorder
BPD	Bronchopulmonary Dysplasia
CF	Cystic Fibrosis
CMV	Cytomegalovirus
CP	Cerebral Palsy
DAPE	Developmental Adapted Physical Education
DCD	Developmental Cognitive Disability
DD	Developmental Disability
ECSE	Early Childhood Special Education
E/BD	Emotional or Behavioral Disorder
ED	Emotional Disorder
FAPE	Free Appropriate Public Education
FAS	Fetal Alcohol Syndrome
HI	Hearing Impaired
IDT	Interdisciplinary Team
IEP	Individualized Education Plan
IFSP	Individual Family Service Plan
IQ	Intelligence Quotient
LD	Learning Disability
LRE	Least Restrictive Environment
MMMI	Mild - Moderate Mentally Impaired
MSMI	Moderate - Severe Mentally Impaired
MD	Muscular Dystrophy
MS	Multiple Sclerosis
NTD	Neural Tube Defect
OHD	Other Health Disability
PI	Physically Impaired
SMI	Severely Multiply Impaired
SLD	Specific Learning Disability
SLP	Speech or Language Pathologist
TBI	Traumatic Brain Injury
VI	Visually Impaired

Section III

Modifications
and
Adaptations

Language Arts Strategies

Reading Comprehension Strategies

Good readers are able to visualize and form images in their minds to help them understand what they are reading. Poor readers, however, are unable to do this and experience extreme difficulty with understanding what they are reading. These readers are spending their time decoding and sounding out words and may forget to pay attention to what the words are telling them. Graphic organizers, as described below, are visual depictions of the events and happenings in a story. The graphic organizers are used to assist students in comprehending what they read.

1. Story charts or maps

Identify the characters, setting, problem, sequence of events, and the resolution of conflict of a story read by using charts and maps. Primary grades will use a slightly modified chart compared to the chart used by the upper elementary grade levels. (See examples on pages 60 and 61).

2. Storyboard

Divide the chalkboard or a piece of paper into sections (6-8 sections depending on the length of the story). Have the students draw, write, or dictate for the teacher to record the story events in sequence in each box or section. (See example on page 62).

3. Plot profiles

After reading a book or story, choose a number of events and produce a class graph of which events students found to be the most exciting. Plot on a large graph the majority opinion of the class regarding how exciting each event was. (Have the students show hands or applaud when you mention the part of the story that they thought was most exciting.)

5. Wanted posters

Have the students create posters by drawing a picture of and writing about identifying characteristics of a character in the book.

6. Venn diagrams

Use the circular diagram to compare and contrast two similar books, stories, or pieces of literature. Compare two versions of a story, a book with its movie version, or two characters within a book.

7. Character web

Put the character's name in the center of the web and then have students report traits and descriptions of that character in the outer sections of the web. (See example on page 63).

Story Chart

Use this chart to identify the different elements of the story you just read.

Title:
Author:
Illustrator:
Characters:
Setting:
Problem:
Solution:

Story Chart

Use the chart to identify the different elements of the story you just read. You can draw a picture or write words to describe the elements.

Title:
Author:
Illustrator:
Characters:
Setting:
Story Summary:

Storyboard

Draw pictures or write sentences about the story events in the order the events occur.

Story Title _____
Author _____
Illustrator _____

1.	2.
3.	4.
5.	6.

Character Web

Write the character's name in the center of the web. Write the character's traits and describe the character in the outer sections of the web.

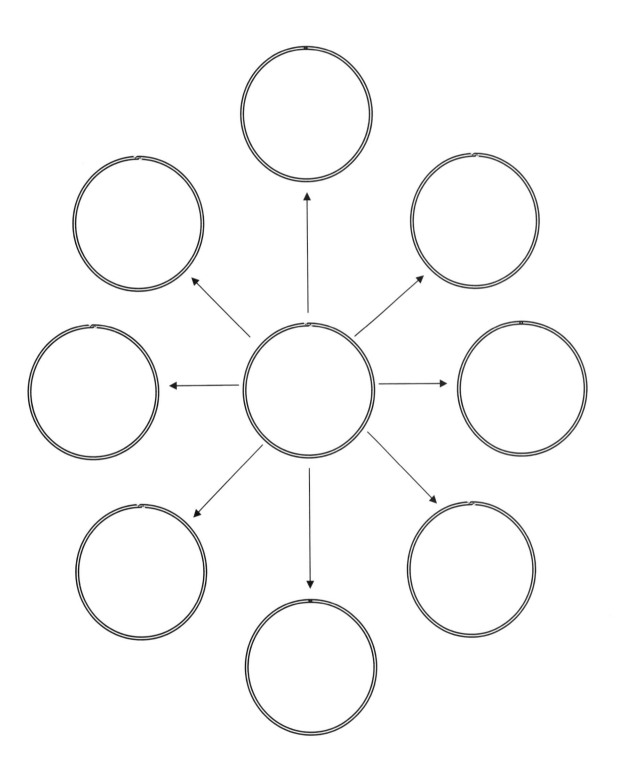

Oral Reading Strategies

Students who experience difficulty with reading often have a hard time following along and paying attention. These students frequently lose their place in the passage, and thus lose the meaning of the words they are reading. Oral reading is extremely difficult for some students. Often, students with poor oral reading skills are so afraid of the embarrassment they believe they will experience when reading aloud that they will lose the meaning of the whole passage. Here are some oral reading strategies to try in order to avoid frustration and panic from those who struggle with reading orally.

1. Teacher reads out loud.

The teacher orally reads the story first, modeling for fluency, expression, and interest while the students follow along with their own copy of the selection. (Require younger students to point to each word while you are reading.)

2. Students read silently before orally.

Give the students a chance to read the selection silently before being asked to read orally. Students who are uncomfortable reading orally (particularly older students) should never be forced to read out loud to the class. They should be able to volunteer when they wish to read in front of the class. Buddy reading or reading is small groups rather than in front of the whole class is a "safer," preferable way for students to practice their oral reading.

3. Volunteers or student aides assist children with reading.

Have student aides or volunteers (parents, grandparents, etc.) listen to the children read. Provide a brief training session for the volunteers. Explain how and when they should provide assistance to the students.

4. Use buddy or partner reading.

Assign each student a buddy or partner. It is beneficial to strategically place the confident readers with those who struggle. Before attempting to partner read for the first time, explain to students how to help one another. Also explain when to intervene so that one partner does not do all of the reading while the struggling student becomes a bystander.

Give each student a chance to read the story individually first and explain that the partners will take turns reading orally and listening to their buddy read. Explain in advance how many paragraphs or sentences a student is to read before changing partners. When possible, allow students to share one book; however, for distractible students, it may be better for each student to use his or her own copy of the book.

Buddies can take turns or can read in unison. You may want to assign questions to each pair, so the students know what they will be responsible to answer at the end of the session. This also provides a purpose for reading. Separate the students into their own space so they are not distracted by other groups.

Spelling Strategies

Students are poor spellers for many reasons. Some students are inattentive to visual details while others struggle to recall the combination of letters. A number of students may be visually unaware of word patterns or may reverse letters such as the letter *b* for *d*. A few students are simply careless in their writing and spelling resulting in numerous errors. Here are some suggestions that may help students with spelling.

Spelling Practice Activities

1. Teach high-frequency words.
High frequency words should be top priority in your spelling instruction. It is said that about half of the English language is composed of the 100 most frequently used words. One thousand words account for over 90% of words frequently used in everyday writing.

2. Have the students write the words in the air, using large movements.
Ask the students to say the letters out loud as they write the word in the air.

3. Write words using glitter and glue or starch on a piece of cardboard.
Students may sprinkle glitter, sand, salt, or any powdery material over the top of the glue or starch. Once it dries, it creates a textured, 3-D spelling word which can be used for tactile practice of tracing the words.

4. Provide a tray of sand or salt.
Have students write the spelling words with their finger in the sand or salt while spelling out loud.

5. "Finger-paint" spelling words.
Squirt shaving cream on the desktop for student to practice writing words. You may also spread a small amount of pudding, frosting, or whipped cream on a paper plate. Once the word is written, the student can erase it by smoothing over the "cream" and then proceed to write the next word.

6. Pair students.
Students may use their fingers to trace their spelling words on their partner's back or they can orally spell the words back and forth between partners. Older students may take turns quizzing one another.

7. Use individual chalkboards or whiteboards.
This activity may be used as a whole group activity. Supply the students with colored chalk for chalkboards or colored pens for whiteboards. Once the spelling words are written, count to three and ask the students to hold

up the boards so you are able to make a quick check of individual spelling boards. If using chalk, students may store their chalk in a sock. The student will have his or her chalk and "eraser" in one place.

8. Use a clean paintbrush and water.

Students may practice writing words on a chalkboard or desktop.

9. Use manipulative letters.

Provide students with magnetic letters, alphabet cookies, sponge letters, rubber stamps, or stencils to use for individual practice of the words.

10. Play games.

Create various games that incorporate the spelling words. Games such as Scrabble®, Wheel of Fortune®, and Boggle® will help with spelling. Students may create crossword puzzles, word finds, and play games such as hangman. Small groups of students may quiz one another orally or have mini-spelling bees.

11. Make use of technology.

Computer spelling programs are often enjoyed by students. Weekly spelling lists may be inserted into the program. For students who have difficulty with spelling, a spell checker will help with written assignments but will not replace the need for spelling instruction.

12. Use configuration clues.

Print a word and then outline its shape in a different color. This will help students to recognize the use of tall letters and letters which go below the bottom line.

13. Use memory aids with spelling.

Memory aids help with spelling. Ask students to create their own. Some common examples include:

The princi<u>pal</u> is a <u>pal</u>.	I will have <u>2</u> de<u>ss</u>erts, please.
<u>Ron</u> studied the envi<u>ron</u>ment.	No one bel<u>ie</u>ves a <u>lie</u>.
I before E, except after C.	A fri<u>end</u> is a fri<u>end</u> to the <u>end</u>.
Q is always followed by u.	<u>Here</u> is in the words w<u>here</u> and t<u>here</u>.

When two vowels go walking, the first one does the talking.

14. Have students practice only the words that are misspelled on the pretest.

It is more efficient to focus only on the misspelled words for spelling practice. For some students the weekly list may need to be modified if the student misses the majority of words on the pretest.

Strategies for Testing Spelling Skills

1. Pronounce each word slowly.

Slowly say the individual sounds of each word when dictating the spelling words. This helps students hear the sequence of the sounds as they spell.

2. Provide adequate time.

Allow students the time they need to write the word down carefully, before going on to the next word. Also, provide additional time after the test to go over and finish writing words that weren't completed at first.

3. Provide shortened spelling lists.

Spelling lists may need to be modified for students who experience significant difficulties with spelling. Provide "extra credit" for any words beyond the shortened list that students may study and attempt to spell during a test.

4. Allow students to take tests orally.

Have students take a written test and an oral test. Use whichever score is higher.

5. Consider letter reversal.

For students who continually reverse letters, carefully analyze the final test. If there are numerous letter reversals, ask the student to spell the word orally. The goal of a spelling test is to test spelling, not written language.

Handwriting Strategies

Some students have trouble writing neatly on or within the given lines of a piece of paper. Letters may be formed incorrectly and their written work may look disorganized and sloppy. Many students write too quickly causing their handwriting to be unreadable. Others, however, write very slowly to produce their best work, which may take too much time to complete an assignment; therefore the work is incomplete. It is often found that the cause of incorrect handwriting is that the student has never learned proper letter formation strokes. The student may have been inattentive or not ready to learn when beginning handwriting was taught. Thus, the student has created their own unique way of letter formation. Unfortunately, once letters are learned incorrectly, it is very difficult to break students of these habits. Often when a student has found his or her own way of writing, it will become permanent. This emphasizes the importance of consistent and correct teaching in the early primary school years. If you have a student struggling with handwriting difficulties, try some of the following suggestions.

1. Carefully teach and model new letters for the student.

Show the strokes as you talk through the steps of forming the letters.

2. Consistently require students to correct mistaken letters in all written work.

Bring students' attention to letter reversals and incorrectly formed letters in all assignments. Assist students in correcting their mistakes.

3. Demonstrate letters using large movements in the air.

Talk through the strokes and formation of the letters as you practice writing the letters in the air. Have student write the letters in the air also. Watch each student to ensure that each is making the correct stokes.

4. Always observe while students are practicing.

Walk around the room and identify students in need of one-on-one, small group assistance, and students who need immediate re-teaching. The continual monitoring is very important as once a student learns and practices and incorrect letter formation, it is almost impossible to break the students' habit.

5. Provide students special materials.

Pencil Grips: Placing a grip on the pencil may help the student to hold the pencil more easily. Older students may use tape or a rubber band.

Pencil Types: Thick beginner pencils may help some students. As the student become older, experiment with using flair pens, mechanical pencils, and ball point pens.

Paper: Use a paper that is comfortable for the student. Some students will need to use wide ruled paper which may be different than that used be their peers. Computer paper with alternating green and white lines will help some students with correct formation of letters. Paper with raised lines is useful for students who have difficulty staying within the lines when writing. Graph paper will help students who have spatial problems.

Written Expression Strategies

Writing is very difficult for many students, especially when they are expected to "just write." For many, determining a topic about which to write and then gathering ideas about that topic are very troublesome. These students struggle to place their ideas on paper in an interesting and descriptive way. Here are some strategies to try with kids who have difficulty with this in your class.

1. Develop a list of topics of interest.

As a class, brainstorm a list of topics that would be of interest for students to write about. Some examples may include sports, scary things, vacation places, current events, favorite things to do, or hobbies. This class list that can be posted in the classroom to serve as an idea generator when students are expected to write in journals or any other writing activity. When students say "I don't know what to write about," you can direct them to the list.

2. Use semantic mapping.

This strategy will help students to organize their thoughts before they begin writing. Place the main topic in the center of the paper. Place subcategories around the main topic and then add details pertaining to the subcategories. The character web on page 63 may be used.

3. Give alternatives to over-used words.

Generate a class word list or word bank of over-used, boring words (1-cent words) that can be substituted for more interesting words (10-cent words and 25-cent words). Use a thesaurus to have students find "more valuable" words.

1-Cent	10-cents	25-cents
run	race	sprint
	dash	scramble
	speed	hasten
fast	hasty	swift
		speedy

4. Teach descriptive language.

Post examples of metaphors, similes and other descriptive language found in literature. Encourage students to find examples of the various types of descriptive language in their reading. Provide time during each week for students to share the examples they have found.

5. Show, don't just tell.

Teach students to create a picture or scene using words.

Have students close their eyes and ask them to think of a scene or picture with which they are familiar. Have students describe the image orally and then in writing. The student should describe what the scene feels, tastes, looks, and sounds like. Encourage students to think about and use all of their senses to assist in writing descriptively.

Have students chose a photograph, magazine picture, postcard, or illustration from a story. Ask the students to write a descriptive paragraph about the selected picture. When students have finished writing, display all of the pictures around the classroom. Randomly pass out the paragraphs to all students. Have each student read their given paragraph and then try to match the paragraph with the picture that was described. If you have a student who is unable to write, ask the student to orally describe the picture to the class or have the student dictate their description to you or a peer, while it is written for them.

6. Keep a writing folder for all students.

Each student should have a writing folder available for personal use. The student may use this folder to write down their thoughts or ideas. Later these ideas may be used as topic ideas or free write ideas for later assignments.

7. Use neighborhood pen pals.

Arrange opportunities with other teachers to share writing between classrooms. The students may write notes or letters to students in another classroom in the same school, or different local schools. Neighborhood pen pals works well as the response is often received within a couple of days, whereas with distant pen pals, the time period between letters may take several weeks to a month.

8. Use a daily journal.

Students need daily opportunities to practice writing for fluency and consistency. Journals should not be graded. When using journals, it is best to provide a specific period of time on a daily basis. Often, teachers use the beginning of transition time period (such as when the students arrive to class, after a lunch break, or after physical activity such as physical education or recess). It may be beneficial to provide sentence starters or journal prompts for those who find it difficult to independently choose a topic.

Buddy Journal: Provide each of your students with a writing buddy from their classroom or a collaborating classroom at the same grade level. The writing buddies may utilize the journal as a way to converse with each other through reading and writing. One buddy writes into the journal passes it along to the buddy. The buddy reads it, responds, and directs questions and comments back to the first buddy.

Secret Buddy Journal: Instead of using names, a number is assigned to each journal. The student communicates with his or her "secret" buddy. The journals are passed between classrooms, and the students continue to communicate with one another trying to guess who their secret buddy is. Students may describe themselves, describe their likes and dislikes and share information without using their names.

Written Mechanics Strategies

Students who struggle academically are often very weak in the mechanics of language. They struggle to seek and find their own errors and to self-correct their written work. Try some of these strategies with students who struggle with the mechanics of writing.

1. Provide frequent reminders.
Students need to be reminded frequently to check their work for capitalization and punctuation errors. You may want to post a checklist in the classroom which students may refer to when proofing their final papers.

2. Use questioning techniques to help students find their own errors.
Teacher: "What two things do all sentences need?"
Student: "A capital letter at the beginning and an ending punctuation mark."
Teacher: "Does your sentence have both of those things?"

3. Frequently model how to edit and find mechanical errors.
Provide students with examples of work with mechanical errors. As a class, correct the errors by walking through the passage step by step. Be sure to explain why the specific examples are erroneous.

4. Let students edit each other's work.
This works well, as students are often more observant with other's work than with their own.

5. Dictate to students.
Provide one or two sentences orally for the students to write. Ask each student to add the correct punctuation and capital letters. When students have finished with their corrections, write the sentence correctly on the overhead or board, and ask the students check their work. Ask the students, "Do your sentences look like mine?"

6. Provide short written samples for students to correct.
The sentences may also be written on the board or overhead for the students to copy. The written sentences should not contain any capital letters or punctuation. Have the student copy the sentences into a notebook or journal and add the correct punctuation. Then have the students take turns making the corrections on the model and explaining why each correction was made. Students may correct their own work samples. One or two sentences daily are sufficient.

7. Have the student dictate a few sentences.

Copy exactly what the student says onto a chart. Be sure that all students are watching as you are writing what is being said. As you record the student sentences verbatim, omit the capital letter and punctuation in the sentences. Have students identify the errors in the sentences. Always require students to explain the reason for the correction. It is important to continually repeat the rules of written mechanics, as it will help students to become more familiar with the rules and transfer it to their own writing.

8. Create checklists to help students review daily written assignments.

Following are three examples of proofreading checklists which will help students to check their own work. Create individual checklists and photocopy them for your students. The checklists should include the appropriate written language goals for your grade level. The students may keep the checklist at their desks or clip it to a final paper to show that they have proofread the assignment.

Examples of proofreading checklists.

Capital Letters	□ beginning of sentences □ names □ specific places □ title of story
Punctuation	□ . □ ? □ !
Spelling	□ dictionary □ notes

□ **Spelling**	□ Spelling
□ **Punctuation**	□ Punctuation
□ **Capital Letters**	□ Appearance

□ **Paragraphs**
  □ **indented**
  □ **topic sentence**
  □ **details**
	□ Capitalization
	
	□ Error Analysis

□ **Margins**	The word **SPACE** is used as an acronym to help students remember the five items in the proofing list
□ **Overall Appearance**	
□ **Name, Date, Class Period**	

Reprinted with permission from <u>Inclusion: An Essential Guide for the Paraprofessional</u> C. 2003 Peytral Publications Inc.

Math Strategies

Often, students who typically struggle with academics have exhibited learning strengths in spatial awareness, logical thinking, reasoning, and/or visualization. They have the ability to excel in a balanced mathematics curriculum which emphasizes patterns, geometry, measurement, probability, and logic. These students need hands-on activities and may benefit from using manipulatives (pattern blocks, base-ten blocks, interlocking cubes, cubes, or tiles) graphing activities, searching for patterns, and using other non-textbook, non-worksheet type strategies. It is important that the emphasis of mathematics is not placed on assigning students problem after problem or page after page of tedious computation.

Computation Strategies

1. **Evaluate the student's math skills in alternate ways.**
   If using the traditional paper/pencil test, allow additional testing time for students that need it. Consider alternative forms of testing such as a take-home test, computer-assisted assessments, math portfolios, or a project, or give credit if the student is able to demonstrate knowledge of the process.

2. Provide cubes, buttons, counters, or other concrete objects.

Allow students to utilize materials that will assist them with the problem-solving process. Manipulative objects may include any items that can be counted or will convey a quantity. As the student understands the process, the student will be able to move from the concrete to the conceptual level.

Number squares may be used to help students see patterns. They are helpful for students who have difficulty with number concepts. Number squares may be used to show patterns or to teach even/odd numbers, addition, subtraction, multiplication, and division. The following number square is a visual picture of counting by fives or multiples of five. The following page includes two different number squares which may be photocopied for student use.

1	2	3	4		6	7	8	9	
11	12	13	14		16	17	18	19	
21	22	23	24		26	27	28	29	
31	32	33	34		36	37	38	39	
41	42	43	44		46	47	48	49	
51	52	53	54		56	57	58	59	
61	62	63	64		66	67	68	69	
71	72	73	74		76	77	78	79	
81	82	83	84		86	87	88	89	

Number Squares

1	2	3	4	5	6	7	8	9	10
11	12	13	14	15	16	17	18	19	20
21	22	23	24	25	26	27	28	29	30
31	32	33	34	35	36	37	38	39	40
41	42	43	44	45	46	47	48	49	50
51	52	53	54	55	56	57	58	59	60
61	62	63	64	65	66	67	68	69	70
71	72	73	74	75	76	77	78	79	80
81	82	83	84	85	86	87	88	89	90
91	92	93	94	95	96	97	98	99	100

1	2	3	4	5	6	7	8	9	10
11	12	13	14	15	16	17	18	19	20
21	22	23	24	25	26	27	28	29	30
31	32	33	34	35	36	37	38	39	40
41	42	43	44	45	46	47	48	49	50
51	52	53	54	55	56	57	58	59	60
61	62	63	64	65	66	67	68	69	70
71	72	73	74	75	76	77	78	79	80
81	82	83	84	85	86	87	88	89	90
91	92	93	94	95	96	97	98	99	100

3. Provide Touch Math® strategies.

Touch Math® is available from Innovative Learning. It may be used as a complete program or as a supplement to regular mathematics instruction. The program strategically places "touch points" on numerals 1 – 9. Students memorize these points. The program will help students add (counting forward) and subtract (counting back). It may also be used for multiplication.

4. Permit and encourage the use of calculators.

If students are struggling with computational aspects, allow them to use calculators, once each student has demonstrated that the concept is understood. The number square concept presented in idea #2 is an alternative to calculator use if a student has difficulty with basic computation.

5. Provide students with various paper options.

When working on problems that require the students to demonstrate their work, allow them to record their work on regular notebook paper with two or three lines of space between problems. Lined notebook paper turned sideways, or wide-width graph paper may be used.

6. Assign an appropriate number of problems.

In an attempt to determine whether or not a student grasps a specific mathematical concept or to provide practice on the concept, there is little value in assigning an entire page of math calculations if the struggling student is able to demonstrate mastery by completing 40-50% of the calculations.

7. Avoid the stress of timed tests of basic facts.

Many students struggle with the memorization of basic addition, subtraction, multiplication, and division facts. Often, when given time to think, the student is well aware of the basic facts; however, the essence of the "timed test" contributes anxiety, causing the student to perform poorly on the timed test. Struggling students may be expected to complete the same test; however, do not require it to be completed in a specific amount of time. Also, give credit to the student who responds orally and/or the student who needs to rely on manipulatives. Students are learning when they understand the process of how to arrive at the answer of a mathematical problem. The student should not be penalized if it takes a longer period of time to complete the process.

8. Reduce the amount of copying.

Provide students who struggle with photocopied pages of assignments. Allow another person (aide, parent, or volunteer) to help by copying the problems onto paper for the student.

9. Highlight processing signs.

Highlighting math symbols will draw attention to the mathematical operation necessary for successful completion of the problem. Many students are not attentive to operational signs on a page, especially if they change frequently (for example between addition and subtraction).

10. Color or highlight the ones column.

Draw attention to where the student is supposed to begin working on the problem.

11. Provide students with only one worksheet at a time.

Avoid overwhelming students with too many pages at one time.

12. Visually list all the steps for each process.

Write the steps for the different mathematical processes and have them posted throughout the room for students to refer to when needed. Students may also create small books containing the steps in the process, to keep in their math folders and use at home.

13. Use whiteboards and overhead projectors for teaching mathematical concepts.

Utilize overhead transparent manipulatives such as calculators, pattern blocks, and cubes in daily teaching. Students often grasp materials when they can visually see as well as hear how to work through a specific process.

14. Keep the copying of math problems from the board or overhead to a minimum.

Struggling students may have difficulty copying assignments from the board or overhead. Keep in mind that math is about number relationships and not about accurate copying.

Test Strategies

Test-Taking (for students)

The word "test" causes extreme anxiety for many students, especially those who struggle with academic requirements. Testing for many students is frequently a frustrating and unsuccessful experience. Here are some important suggestions to help students become more comfortable with their test-taking skills. You may want to teach the skills at the beginning of the school year and then review them with students before each test.

Teach students to recognize the types of test formats used. Often, more than one format is used within a test. Once the format is determined, the following steps will assist students in answering the questions as accurately as possible.

Multiple Choice Format

1. Read through the question. Try to answer to the question, if possible, before reading the multiple choices provided.

2. If you are able to answer the question, read through the choices and find the answer that most closely parallels your answer.

3.   If you are unsure of the answer to the question, proceed to the next question. Do not spend time at the beginning of the test attempting to answer questions of which you are unsure.

4.   Once you have answered the questions that you are sure of, go back to answer the rest of the questions.

5.   When answering a question that you are unsure of, look through the choices given. Cross out the obvious incorrect answers. Try to eliminate at least two answers so that you only have two answers left to choose from.

6.   Once you have narrowed your choices to two and still are uncertain, select the answer that seems to make the most sense.

Matching Format

1.   Read through both columns of information completely before attempting to make any matches.

2.   Answer the items that you are sure of by matching those first.

3.   Cross out all choices once you have used them. (Be certain that the answers are only going to be used one time each before crossing them out.) Cross them out lightly in case you later change your mind and need to erase.

4.   Once you have made all matches that you are certain of and crossed out all coordinating matches, go back to complete all remaining matches.

5.   If you are uncertain of which matches to make with the remaining choices, make a choice that would make the best sense to you.

6.   After all matches are made, go back and check to be sure that you have used all matching choices from both columns.

Fill-in-the-Blank Format

1.   Read through all the questions first. Answer all questions of which you are confident. If a word bank is provided, cross out answers that you have used.

2.   Use only key words in the blank.

3. Once you have answered all questions that you are sure of, refer to other items in the test to see if they will provide you with useful information to assist in answering the remaining questions.

4. If you are uncertain of the answer, make a choice that would make the best sense to you.

Essay Format

1. Read all of the essay questions entirely before attempting to answer any of them.

2. Once you have read all of the essay questions, choose the easiest one to answer first.

3. Once you have selected the one to answer first, write down all facts that you feel are essential to answer the question. Put the facts in an order that will assist you in answering the question. Use the written facts to help you write the essay.

4. After completing the question, re-read it carefully to be sure that what you have written aligns with what the question is asking for. Be sure that you have answered all parts of the question.

Test Writing (for teachers)

Before the test:

1. **Allow time in class to review.**
    Provide a study guide for students. Allow time during class, prior to administering the test, to review the information on the study guide. Provide games or review activities for students to participate in. Include the information that will be on the test.

2. **Provide a review test.**
    This is essential, especially if students are unfamiliar with the format of the test. Allow students time to practice with multiple-choice, fill-in-the-blank, matching, and essay formats. Students also need to know what is expected of them. Allow students to take the study guide home two or three nights before the test in order to study at home as well.

The Test:

1. **Organize and format the test carefully.**
    Be sure that the test is written so all students can read it. Most students are able to read typed print; however, if you are unable to type the test, be sure to print it. Do not write a test in cursive, as not all students can read cursive handwriting. Be sure that adequate white space is left on the paper. Tests which have test items crowded onto a page often seem overwhelming to the struggling student. Two pages with appropriately spaced questions will seem less intimidating for students than one page that is crowded with very little visible white space.

2. **Allow students to respond orally.**
    If a student feels more comfortable testing orally, and if time permits, allow the student to do so. Ask the student to give the answer to an assistant while the assistant writes the answer verbatim. The student may also respond orally and tape record the response. If time is available, the student may share the answers directly with you. You will have a better understanding of the students' knowledge base if the student who has difficulty with fine motor and written language is allowed to respond orally.

3. **Allow the test to be read to the student.**
    If a student struggles with reading decoding but understands the conceptual material being assessed on the test, the teacher will get a much more accurate assessment of the student's knowledge if the test is read to the student.

4. **Provide shortened tests.**
    This should be used only for students who will become overwhelmed by longer tests. This will be noted in the student's IEP, as the final outcome is different than the student's peer group.

5. **Clarify the test directions.**
    Be sure the student understands the directions. Make sure you are available during the test to answer the student's questions.

Transition Strategies

Transition and non-instructional times during the day are often challenging times for students. Here are some ways to help avoid behavior difficulties during unstructured times.

1. Inform students of any upcoming changes in the daily schedule.

Try to avoid surprises in the routine. If there is an assembly, guest speaker, substitute teacher, or other change in routine, inform students who have difficulty with transitions in advance.

2. Discuss what will happen and teach the specific behaviors that are required for each new situation.

Use techniques such as role-playing and practicing of specific behaviors before introducing a new situation to the students.

3. Use flashing lights, the ringing of a bell, or some sort of a cue to inform students that an activity will soon be ending.

Be consistent with the cues used during transition times so that students are familiar with them and always know what it means when you utilize the cue. A two-minute warning is often appropriate, as it forewarns the student of the upcoming conclusion to a project.

4. Allow a short rest time, exercise, or some sort of "down-time" between structured activities.

This will help students to get some of their "wiggles" and excess energy out before moving on to the next activity.

5. Be prepared to physically help a student through a transition time.

This is very helpful for the student who struggles with transition times. Close proximity to the student is often beneficial and serves as a reminder to help the student remain "in control."

6. Provide whole-class incentives when smooth transitions occur.

There are a variety of ways to do this. The entire class may be rewarded with a point when the transition is smooth. A goal may be set and, once the class meets the goal the entire class is rewarded. Rewards may include extra free time, a video, outside time or whatever reward the class would like to work towards.

Attention

Getting It

1. Provide a signal to get students' attention.

Turn off, flash the lights, ring a bell, clap, or raise your hand to signal to students that you need their attention.

2. Use different tones and volume of your voice.

Use loud, soft, and whispering voices. Try using a consistent chant or action to get attention such as, "Clap once" (children clap once), and "Clap twice" (children clap twice). Children should know that voices should be off after clapping twice. Once there has been silence, you can continue in a normal voice to give directions.

3. Use eye contact.

Always ensure that you have eye contact with your students before providing instruction. Student must learn that if they are in a position where they are unable to maintain eye contact they should move to a position where they are able to see you. Students should be instructed to turn their chairs or bodies towards you during instruction time.

4. Always show excitement and enthusiasm about the lessons and activities that are being taught.

If students see that you are excited about what the upcoming lessons and activities, they will tend to become interested and excited as well.

5. Do what it takes to get attention, even if it means being silly.

Sometimes using props or dressing in costume will help to get the students attention and interest about the upcoming lesson.

6. Be Mysterious.

Inside a box or bag, place an item that is related to the upcoming lesson. Show students the box or bag and encourage them to guess or predict what they think is inside the box or bag. This will keep their excitement and interest about the upcoming lesson.

Maintaining It

1. Use visualization.

Write important, key information on the board, on transparencies, or on the overhead.

2. Add color to presentations.

Use colored chalk or pens to highlight the important information and key points on the chalkboard or overhead. Write individual steps to mathematical problems, vocabulary, key words, spelling words, phonics rules, and so forth in different colors.

3. Draw the students' attention to important information.

Point out important information to students both visually and verbally. Verbal clues such as "remember this" or "this is important" will help direct attention. Highlight or frame information with a colored square on transparencies or with your hands when using the board.

4. Use your finger, pointing stick, knitting needle, or conductor's baton to point out specific information.

This will help to focus the students' attention on the important information. The overhead projector allows you to write the important information in color, and allows you to face the students while doing so. The overhead projector improves classroom management by helping to reduce behavior problems. Students enjoy participating in activities which use the overhead projector.

5. Use a flashlight or a lighted pointer.

It is very easy to gain students' attention when the lights are turned off and a flashlight or lighted pointer is used to highlight important information.

6. Utilize hands-on materials and activities whenever possible.

Actively involve students in the learning process whenever appropriate.

7. Use a pleasant but firm voice.

Be sure that you can be clearly heard by all students. Tape record and analyze your lectures. Do you speak clearly? Too quickly? Too slowly?

8. Keep the lesson easily understandable.

Teach lessons at a quick pace, but be sure to frequently check for understanding. Monitor and adjust the lessons as needed.

9. Be prepared.

Teaching a lesson takes preparation on your part. When you are prepared and all materials are at hand, the down time during the lesson is decreased. Students are less likely to be disruptive when they are on-task.

10. Help the students to record important information.

For some students, note-taking is very difficult. Students can practice by taking brief notes during all class lectures. Point out the most important information so the student writes it down. Allow time at the end of the class for the students to compare notes and write additional information which they may have missed.

11. Call on students with equity.

Teachers tend to unintentionally ignore or refrain from calling on certain students in the classroom. Most often, teachers are unaware that certain students are overlooked. Some teachers tend to call on females more frequently than males or vice versa. Some teachers are more apt to call on the students who usually provide the correct information. At times teachers purposefully call on students who they think are unsure of the answer or call on students who have not been paying attention. Students quickly learn their teachers' habits and can often predict their chances of being called on. Students who perceive that they will be required to contribute and speak in front of their peers will remain more attentive.

Try some of these suggestions to assist with greater equity:

Write each student's name on an index card. When a student response is needed, pull a name from the deck of cards and call on that student. Replace the card in the deck and shuffle the cards. The possibility exists that the student will be called upon again.

Write each student's name on a popsicle stick and place the sticks in a cup. During group activity select a popsicle stick. Place the stick back into the cup, making it possible for that student to be called on again.

Ask students to write their name on the top of an index card and to make a tally mark on the card each time they are called upon during class. Explain to the students that you are trying to be more consistent and want to be sure that all students have an opportunity to participate during class. At the end of the predetermined time, collect the cards to evaluate your pattern of student's selection.

12. Wait, wait, and wait!

When directing questions to individual students, allow sufficient wait time so the student is able to process the question, gather his or her thoughts, and formulate an answer to the question. While waiting for a student to answer, slowly count to five before rephrasing the question or calling on another student.

13. Allow for special circumstances.

Be sensitive to students who are often viewed by peers as poor students. Help these students feel more comfortable responding to and answering questions during class. Tell the student to raise his hand with a fist closed or first finger pointing up when he thinks he knows the answer but is not sure. If the student is quite certain of the answer, he can raise an open hand and signal you to call on him on those occasions.

Whole-Group Response

Periodically check for understanding of concepts by using whole group response methods. Whole-group responses help students to be actively involved in the learning process.

1. Use individual whiteboards or chalkboards.
Provide small chalkboards or whiteboards to students. As a question is directed to the class, each student writes the individual response on the board. Allow sufficient time for the students to respond in writing. Once the students have written their responses, count to three and ask the students to display their answers by holding the board under their chins. This allows the teacher to quickly view the answer and determine which students understand the concept and which students need remediation.

2. Have students answer in unison.
Hold up an open hand and ask the class a question. Explain to students that when your hand is raised and open, it means students are to be listening and not speaking. After asking the question, allow time for the students to process the question and formulate their answers. On the count of three, close your hand to a fist, signaling the students to call out the answer in unison.

3. Use the point/tap method.
This method works well for drilling on new vocabulary words or spelling words. The location of the pointer indicates how the student is to respond. If your finger, the pointer, the chalk, or the pen is pointing to the left side of the word, the student should read the word silently. As the pointer is moved to the right side of the word, students should say the word out loud, in unison. Be sure and allow time for the students to process the word before asking for a unison response.

4. Use yes/no whole class responses.
The most effective way to use yes/no whole-class response is through hand signals and colored cards. When hand signals or cards are used, the student should indicate his response close to the chin or their body so that other students are unable to see their response. Some types of yes/no, whole-class responses may include:
- Thumbs up / thumbs down
- Open hand / closed hand
- Red card / green card
- Happy face / sad face
- Lead end / eraser end (of a pencil)

Keeping Students On-Task

1. Continually check for understanding.
Before asking students to work independently, be sure that all directions are clear and understood by the students.

2. Give a manageable amount of work.
Be sure the amount of work given to a student is not too demanding or overwhelming. This may mean that the assignment needs to be modified for some students.

3. Model and reinforce on-task behavior.
Always define the on-task behavior during reinforcement ("I like the way John is sitting quietly at his desk and working on his assignment.")

4. Set a time limit.
This works well for students who enjoy the challenge of a "beat-the-clock" system for getting work done. This is neither effective nor appropriate for all students.

5. Seat students who model appropriate, on-task behavior in the proximity of the student who struggles to remain on task.
Often, students who have difficulty staying on task benefit from good role modeling. Good role models also help to reduce the chance of other students' encouraging inappropriate behaviors.

6. Provide a quiet study space.
A study carrel works well for the student who is easily distracted by objects, noises, movement, and events. Try providing the student with a headset (with or without music playing) in order to decrease the classroom noises that may distract the student.

7. Use contracts, behavior charts, or other behavior modification systems.
This works well to encourage on-task behavior.

8. Use response costs and naturally occurring consequences.
This works well for off-task behavior. If students are off task during class time, they can "owe you time" at the end of the day, before school, or for part of recess time. The student must repay the amount of time that he or she was not on task during work time.

9. Use signals or colored signs indicating "I need help!"

Some teachers use a signal (thumbs up or head on desk) or a colored sign that students may place on their desks to alert any adult scanning the room that he or she needs help.

Organization

Homework

1. Assign a peer study buddy to assist the student.

This can be beneficial both for the student requiring assistance and for the peer who is providing the assistance. Be sure when assigning a buddy that the students are able to work together. The study buddy can help the student record homework assignments in a notebook and check to see that the assignments are completed correctly.

2. Require students to use an assignment book.

Provide assignments both verbally and in writing. As you are writing the assignment information on the board or overhead projector, the students should record their assignments in their assignment notebooks at the same time.

3. Take a couple of minutes at the end of every day to review students' homework for that night.

Check to ensure that all students have the appropriate books and school materials need to complete the homework assignments.

4. Let parents know when their child is struggling with homework requirements.

Communication with the parent(s) is important. If the student continually struggles with homework, the parent(s) may need to monitor the homework time. For some students the homework may need to be adjusted.

5. Require students to be prepared for class.

When students arrive unprepared, provide inferior, less desirable materials as substitutions (backside of recycled paper, chewed-up pencils). Do not allow the student to go and retrieve forgotten materials from the locker or storage place as valuable class time is lost. Do not allow students to borrow materials from others. Students need to know that you are serious about your expectations.

6. Check notebooks often.

Reward students for good organization using such things as special certificates, "no homework tonight" passes, and/or special privileges). Have routine checks as well as unannounced checks of notebooks and assignments.

7. Collect all homework.

Designate a specific place for turning in daily assignments. Homework should always be collected or reviewed during class. Be sure students are aware that you will check homework and will hold the student accountable for all homework assignments.

8. Make sure homework is review or practice work.

Do not assign new material as homework. Homework assignments should be review or drill activities that a student will not have to struggle to complete.

9. Listen to comments from parents and students regarding homework completion.

If a parent is concerned because the child is spending many hours each night on homework, consider modifying the requirements and reducing the workload.

10. Color-code textbooks, notebooks, and folders.

When possible try to color-coordinate the required materials for each class. For example, if the main color in the science textbook is blue, ask the student to purchase a blue notebook, folder, and three-ring binder.

11. Provide organizational tools.

Allow students to use a pre-made daily assignment sheet or an organizational materials card to serve as a visual reminder for what as to what they are required to complete. Several organizational checklists and assignment sheets follow. These are easy to create and may be adapted for the individual student. The assignments sheets on the following page may be reproduced.

Did I remember?

	Binder	Books	Materials	Teacher's Initials
Monday				
Tuesday				
Wednesday				
Thursday				
Friday				
Point Total				

Did I remember?

	Pencil	Paper	Book	Teacher's Initials
Monday				
Tuesday				
Wednesday				
Thursday				
Friday				
Point Total				

Daily Assignments

Name: _____

Date: _____

Subject	Assignment	Done	Homework	Done
		☐ Yes ☐ No		☐ Yes ☐ No
		☐ Yes ☐ No		☐ Yes ☐ No
		☐ Yes ☐ No		☐ Yes ☐ No
		☐ Yes ☐ No		☐ Yes ☐ No
		☐ Yes ☐ No		☐ Yes ☐ No

Daily Assignments

Date	Subject Area	Assignment	Due Date	Complete √

Assignment Sheet

SUBJECT AREA	MONDAY	TUESDAY	WEDNESDAY	THURSDAY	FRIDAY
MATH					
SOCIAL STUDIES					
ENGLISH					
SCIENCE					
TESTS					
PROJECTS					
MISC.					

Written Work Organization

1. Teach consistent ways to complete classwork.

Develop consistent guidelines for daily assignments. All assignments should include the student's name, date, subject, and the page number, if applicable. Additional guidelines may require that all assignments are written on notebook paper, skipping every other line. (A sample reference poster with the appropriate format for written assignments is helpful). Once a specific standard is established, require this of all written assignments.

2. Teach students to provide appropriate spacing and avoid crowding on the paper.

Teach beginning writers use the two-finger rule. Students should leave approximately two finger spaces between words decreasing to one space as the student becomes more proficient.

3. Lightly draw left and right margins on paper.

This will help students learn to stay within the boundary lines.

4. Use heavy, thick paper that doesn't rip easily.

Some students need to erase frequently. Heavier paper helps the student avoid torn assignments.

5. Teach letter sizes for handwriting.

Refer to the top line as a "head line", middle line as the "belt line," and the bottom line as a "foot line." When writing letters such as the letter "b," remind students to start at the head line, go all the way down to the foot line, and add a belly at the middle line.

6. Teach organization of math problems on a notebook page.

Encourage students to leave space between individual problems, even if it means additional paper will be used. It may be helpful to provide graph paper for math computation problems. (Write one number in each section of the graph paper to help the student keep track of the place-value columns.) Or, encourage students to use regular notebook paper turned sideways so the lines run vertically instead of horizontally across the page. This will help students keep their columns aligned properly.

7. Require students to use a three-ring binder.

Students in early elementary school can begin to organize their work into a three-ring binder with dividers. Encourage students to place their materials into the correct section and instruct them not to remove the papers until it is time to turn them in.

Time Management

1. Help with independent time management and organization.

Put a clock face or faces on the students' desks. Set the clock so that the hands are pointing to the time that the individual student needs to leave the room for various supplemental services. Also, write time in words and numbers as an extra reminder. Encourage students to remember, on their own, when the time comes to leave the room.

2. Post a daily schedule.

Write the daily schedule on the board or tape a schedule to the student's desk to assist with remembering the different events for the day.

3. Use a 10- or 15-minute time period system.

Anticipate the amount of time a student will need to complete an assignment and set a timer (which should not exceed 15 - 20 minutes). If the assignment is accurately completed within the time frame, reinforcement is provided to the student.

Parental Help with Organization

1. Provide a workplace free of distractions and away from the TV.

Encourage parents to be actively involved during homework times. Parents should not have to help their child with the work (as it should be review or be simple enough for the child to complete alone), but they should be available to answer questions, provide explanations, and provide minimal support if needed.

2. Provide appropriate materials necessary for completing homework.

Be sure the materials used at school are also available at home. If a student needs a ruler or colored pencils in school, the student may also need the same materials at home. If a duplicate set of supplies is available at home, the student will not have to worry about carrying the items from school to home daily.

3. Consistently check your child's assignment notebook.

This works best if this is done at the same time and place each night. For example, your child should know to place his or her assignment notebook on the kitchen table as soon as he or she gets home from school, as you can check it right before supper every night.

4. Help your child to prioritize his or her "to do" list each night.

Some assignments are due daily, whereas others may be long-term assignments. You may want to provide a weekly or monthly calendar so parents are able to help their child prioritize the assignments.

5. Develop and enforce a consistent routine or schedule.

A sample schedule might involve snack, homework, dinner, play, wind down, and bedtime.

6. Help your child pack the backpack for the next day.

Make sure all school materials are in the backpack. It is best to do this before going to bed at night

Strategies for Giving Directions

Make sure all directions you give are clear, concise, and understood by all of your students. The following strategies will help to ensure that your students can successfully follow your directions.

1. Wait until you have everyone's attention.

Wait until all students are completely quiet and students are looking at you before beginning. You may need to provide certain cues to alert students.

2. Explain your expectations as clearly as possible.

Take your time when giving directions, as the extra time spent at the beginning will be beneficial in the end. Be sure all students can see you when you are providing the instructions. Sometimes students pick up cues from your body language.

3. Provide instructions for all learning styles.

Provide both visual and verbal instructions. Write the instructions on the board or overhead while you are giving them orally. Don't erase the directions until the assignment is complete.

4. Show the class what they are to do.

Do not just verbally "tell" the class, but show them as well.

5. Explain each step of the directions slowly and concisely.

Don't just assume that the student understands the direction. For multiple-step directions explain each step individually. To check for understanding, ask the student to repeat the directions back orally.

6. Have students record assignment due dates in their assignment notebooks.
Leave the assignment written on the board until the end of the day. Be sure students understand the difference between the word "do" and "due."

7. Always check for understanding.
Ask for specifics.
Teacher: "What problems do we need to do?"
Class: "Only the odd numbers."

8. Give complete directions.
Be sure to explain what students are expected to do after they have completed the task.

Behavioral Interventions

1. Explain your expectations and requirements.
Make sure the student understands what you are asking of him. Ask the student to repeat the information back to you to check for understanding.

2. Directly teach students what is acceptable and unacceptable.
This needs to be taught for all areas: classroom, hallway, bathroom, lunchroom, computer room, recess, etc. Provide reinforcement for acceptable behavior as well as consequences for unacceptable behavior.

3. Provide structure, routine, predictability, and consistency.
This is true in the classroom as well as in other areas of the school.

4. Allow practice, appropriate modeling, and review of behavioral expectations and rules.

5. Provide clear and fair consequences for all students.

6. Follow through each and every time.
If a student does not follow a specific rule, provide consequences each time. Students need to know that you are serious.

7. Use proactive tactics rather than reactive.
Utilizing proactive reinforcement will minimize the need for reactive consequences.

8. Keep a structured classroom.
Students must know exactly what is expected of them in your classroom. If you are not organized, it will be hard for a student to be organized. If your classroom lacks structure, it will be difficult for students to know what is expected of them.

Behavioral problems often occur during the unstructured times of the day. Creating well-organized lessons and beginning class instruction promptly are generally good deterrents to behavior problems. During transition times such as at the start of the class period, after recess, after physical education, etc., provide the students with a brief assignment to work on when they enter the room. The assignment should be something that is not graded and that can be completed without assistance, such as free-choice reading, journal writing, or spelling practice. This activity ensures that the students have something to work on until you are ready to begin the next activity. Here are some ways to avoid significant behavioral outbreaks by students.

Positive Reinforcement

Positive reinforcement is the best, least restrictive, behavioral management strategy that can be used in the classroom. Positive reinforcement helps to build self-esteem and respect. When you catch students doing what you want them to do, it is important to recognize and consistently praise each specific incident.

- "Thank you, Sally, for raising your hand and waiting to be called on."
- "Joseph, I like the way that you are sitting quietly and waiting for instructions."
- "I like the way that the blue group is using their 'six-inch' voices while they are talking."
- "First graders, it makes me so happy when you are all settled down and waiting to begin our lesson! Thank you!"

Examples of positive reinforcement in the classroom:

1. Acknowledging students' appropriate behavior.
   Acknowledging and praising students is a proactive strategy. This should occur in all settings and at all times.

2. Reward students with classroom jobs and responsibilities.

3. Use major incentives and rewards only when necessary.

4. Allow students to work for tangible or edible rewards.

5. Use some of these additional suggestions for positive reinforcement:
   - Playing a game with a friend
   - Earning "free time"
   - Eating breakfast or lunch with the teacher
   - Reading or looking at magazines
   - Using the computer alone or with a friend
   - Listening to music with a tape recorder and earphones
   - Working with clay, special pens/paper, or whiteboards
   - Skipping an assignment of the student's choice

Classroom Incentives

Classroom incentives are motivators to use for entire classes. The following two suggested incentives can be adapted to meet the needs of any classroom.

1. Students earn tickets or play money.

The tickets or play money may be used towards a weekly, biweekly, or monthly auction or raffle. Students can use their accumulated tickets/money/points to buy assorted toys, items, or privileges.

2. The teacher places marbles, beans, or chips in a jar.

When students are caught doing something well or behaving appropriately the teacher will put a marble, bean or chip in a jar. When the jar is full, the class earns a special party (popcorn, pizza, ice cream), activity (video), or field trip. Students should help to determine the reward activity.

Assertive Discipline

Students must know what will happen when they are following and not following the rules. One way to do this is to use warnings coupled with incremental consequences when students do not follow the rules. When students are following the rules, provide positive attention. Students must know from the beginning what the consequences will be for not following the rules. Various classroom management systems include the following:

1. Color-Coded Cards

This is a system for monitoring behavior of the entire classroom. There are many variations of this system; thus, it can be changed to meet the different needs of the different classrooms. It may involve using a pocket chart with an individual envelope or compartment for each student identified by that student's name. All students start the day with a green card in the envelopes, meaning that every one is ready to GO. When there is a rule infraction, after a WARNING, the color of the individual's card is changed to yellow. This is a warning, indicating that the student must become aware of what is occurring and needs to slow down. With the next rule infraction, the yellow card is changed to the final red or STOP card. This severe consequence may include loss of recess, time away from the class, or a call to a parent. The consequences need to be set up in advance and clearly explained to all students prior to initiating this system.

With this system, students begin each day with a clean slate. For some classes, especially younger ones, it may be wise to start the morning and afternoon with a clean slate. For maximum effectiveness, allow your class to define the consequences associated with the change of each colored card. If you don't want the chart posted for all to see, it is also possible that each student starts the day with a green card at his or her desk. If the card needs to be changed, the teacher can individually and privately go to the student's desk and change the card quietly, with few others noticing. The card may remain in the student's desk or face-down on top of the desk so other students are unaware of the color change.

Another variation of this system is to link each classroom rule to a specific color. When a student breaks a specific rule, the teacher places the color card corresponding to the rule broken into the student's pocket. With this system, the student is clearly aware of the rule that was not followed. The same progressive consequences which were explained above also follow the change of each card.

2. Numbered Cards

If a parent-teacher communication monitoring system would be effective, it can easily be implemented. Prior to starting any system, be sure that the parent(s) are aware of the guidelines. For this behavior system, you will need to make various cards with a number or a number and comment listed (see below). As the end of the day, the student is handed a card to take home.

> 5 - Very well behaved. Great day!
> 4 - Good day
> 3 - So-so day
> 2 - We had some trouble today.
> 1 - We had a very difficult day today.

Students are responsible for making sure a parent sees the notice and then signs it. The student must sign and return the card to school the next school day.

Obviously, not all students will need this type of behavior monitoring, but it has been known to work very well for those who need it and for those who have parents who will support it.

3. Token Economy/ Response Costs

Some teachers use a system of rewards and fines (response cost). For example, using plastic colored links, you could assign a monetary or number value to four colors of the link: yellow = a penny or 1 point, red = a nickel or 2 points, green = a dime or 3 points, and blue = a quarter or 4 points. Specific behaviors are attached to the different point or monetary values as are fines for rule infractions. The teacher "pays" a color link for good behavior. This is the positive reinforcement "token economy" part of the system. When rule infractions occur, the teacher is paid a fine for the specific offense. This is the "response cost" part of the system. It is important to discuss the types of rule infractions that are possible.

This system can be used with an individual student or the entire class. The whole class can earn points and the teacher awards all students a certain value for the links; or individuals can earn points for on-task behavior, not blurting out answers, or whatever target behavior the student is working on.

This token economy/response cost system can be adapted and adjusted to meet the needs of any teacher in any classroom. It is quite effective and not difficult to manage. Examples of rewards for individual students may include pencils, pens, paper, crayons, candy, or any small items. Class rewards may include a video, additional free time, or whatever is mutually decided upon by both the teacher and the class.

Time-Out and Time-Away

Time-out and time-away are appropriate methods to help students to calm down and regain control if the stimulation in the classroom is causing the student to become anxious or out of control. Use time-out and time-away as needed in your classroom. It is important not to view time-out as negative and intrusive. It can be very effective when handled appropriately.

1. Allow the student to remain in the classroom, but away from distractions.
> If a student needs some time-away, a beanbag in the corner of the room, or an empty desk away from the other student desks may provide a quiet area for the student.

2. Send the student to another teacher's classroom.
> Partner up with another teacher (preferably from a different grade level). If a student needs time away, the students can go to the receiving classroom with an independent assignment to work on for a specified amount of time.

3. Allow the student to go to the counselor's office for a few minutes.
> Some students may need someone to talk with. A prearranged location with a social worker or counselor may be appropriate for some students.

Tips for Time-Out and Time-Away

1. Remain calm and positive while you are directing the student to time out.
> For example: "Jesse, I would like for you to sit quietly without making noises. If you can't do that, then go back to your desk. You can join our activity again when you feel you will be able to sit quietly."

2. Try a "think-about-it" chair for a specified amount of time.
> Instruct the student to think about the inappropriate behavior and what they would do differently. A good rule of thumb is one minute of time per year of age. A six-year-old may have about a six-minute time-out.

3. Decide what consequences will be used if the behavior continues after a time-away.

> The majority of students with behavior difficulties will have an alternate plan in place. If the behavior continues the alternate behavior plan should be implemented. The alternate plan may include calling the special education teacher, a counselor, a social worker, or the principal.

4. Ask the student to call a parent at home or in the workplace.

> For some students, a telephone call to the parent often helps.

5. Allow the student to take a "voluntary" time-out if needed.

> As students grow and become more aware of their senses they often can predict when their emotions are escalating to a danger point. In this situation, you may want to create a special pass for the student. The student may use this pass and take a voluntary time-out in the area previously designated. You may want to document the voluntary time-outs to see if they occur at a specific time during the day, during a specific class, or during a specific activity.

6. Do not overuse time-outs.

> Be sure that the student is always aware of the behavior that caused him or her to receive the time-out.

Behavior Contracts

Behavior contracts are agreements between a student and the teacher. A contract must specifically state what behavior is expected and what the reinforcement or reward will be when the behavior/task is completed. Behavior contracts are effective with students. The effectiveness, however, can be short-lived and the rewards/systems may need to be changed frequently. Parental involvement and support is imperative. The behavior contracts on pages 103-104 may be reproduced.

Proximity Control: While circulating in the classroom, try to be near the students with the attention and behavioral problems. Sometimes a hand on the shoulder or establishing eye contact as a quick reminder is effective. It is often helpful to seat children with behavioral or attention difficulties near the teacher or next to a well-focused student. Avoid seating the students near learning centers, the door, windows, or other distracters. Proximity control seems quite simple, and it often has a positive effect on students who need constant reminders to return to task.

Preventative Cueing: This technique helps to prevent disruptive behavior. When the behavior is prevented, it helps the student as there is no confrontation; therefore, the student is not embarrassed in front of his peers. Before beginning this technique, arrange with the student privately a specific hand signal or word signal to use that will help remind the student to calm down, pay attention, stop talking, or change whatever other behavior the student is struggling with. Here are examples of some cueing reminders.

1. Use a traffic light or stop sign signal.

The red light will help to remind students to slow down or stop the behavior. You may also assign instruction to each of the three colors. The red may mean that the students are to be in their seats working, yellow indicates that students may get out of their seats only to ask questions, turn in papers, etc., and the green light means that students may freely move about the classroom.

2. Establish eye contact.

Once you have eye contact touch your eye if you want the student to visually focus on you or you may tug on your earlobe if you would like the student to listen.

3. Use the "thumbs up" sign.

You could use this sign or any other that is agreed upon between you and the student. When the student sees that you are using this sign, he or she can get up and move to another part of the room in order to aid in concentration.

Self-Monitoring: Self-monitoring is one of the least intrusive and least restrictive methods of monitoring one's behavior. With self-monitoring, a target behavior for the student is chosen for the student to record. An example would be thumb-sucking. Every time the teacher or the student "catches" himself sucking his thumb, the student records a tally mark on a slip of paper. At the end of the day, the tally marks are totaled. The teacher and student should have a predetermined reward/response cost system in place. If the student reaches the goal, the reward will be given. If the student does not reach the daily goal, the response cost is issued. Recording one's own behavior is an effective way to increase behaviors such as academic productivity and on-task behavior, or to decrease inappropriate behaviors such as thumb-sucking, talking, or making inappropriate noises.

Planned Ignoring: Planned ignoring is a method used to decrease inappropriate, attention-seeking behaviors. With planned ignoring, the teacher purposefully ignores the behavior, as often the behavior occurs in order to receive the teacher's attention. Obviously, the behavior can only be ignored if it is one that is not destructive to the student or to others. When attempting this strategy, teachers should be aware that the behavior frequently will increase for a short time, as the student will be "testing" to see if he can "make" the teacher pay attention to him. Hang in there! It will get better! Be strong. If the behavior is impacting the education of the other students and it is not improving, however, stop this strategy and attempt another one.

Contract

I _____

agree to _____

_____

_____

_____

My hard work will earn _____

_____

_____

_____

We will meet again to discuss this contract on:_____

_____   _____
Student's Signature   **Date**

_____   _____
Teacher's Signature   **Date**

Contract

I agree to _____

_____

_____

_____

On or before _____

(insert day and date)

If I meet this goal I will earn _____

_____

_____

_____

Signed _____

(student's signature and date)

Signed _____

(teacher's signature and date)

Signed _____

(additional signature if needed)

How Do I Handle This Behavior?

Some students may exhibit behaviors that interfere with others' learning or disrupt the classroom. These behaviors may interfere with the other students' ability to learn. In order for you to successfully manage the classroom, these behaviors need to be decreased. Such behaviors may include continually blurting out answers, making inappropriate noises, falling out of the chair, wandering around the classroom, interrupting you or others during class, or simply engaging in off-task behavior. In the classroom the frequency of such behaviors needs to be decreased in order to have a learning environment in which all students are able to learn. On the other hand, by decreasing the negative behaviors, the positive behaviors such as following directions when asked, completing assignments on time, and on-task behavior will increase.

The following guidelines may be used to decrease unwanted behaviors. The suggestions begin with the least restrictive or intrusive interventions. Depending upon the behavior, the suggestions can be modified or changed to result in the outcome you are trying to achieve.

How to Decrease Inappropriate Behaviors

1. Proximity Control

Place the student's desk next to or in front of your desk. Being physically close to the student will help the student remember to remain in his seat, stay on task, etc.

2. Positive Reinforcement

Reinforce the positive behaviors with verbal praise. Praise the student privately if the student is easily embarrassed by attention. "Wow, Johnny, I haven't seen you get out of your seat (wander around the classroom, be off task, etc.) for 10 minutes. Good for you! Keep it up!"

3. Planned Ignoring

Often times a student will exhibit specific behaviors for attention, even if the attention is negative. Reprimanding the student for negative behaviors may still be reinforcing for the student. Therefore, ignoring the student demonstrates that the student will not get your attention by acting inappropriately. Keep in mind that the behavior may increase for a period of time as the student tries harder to attract your attention. For example, the student who is unable to stay in his seat may begin to fall off of his chair. The student who blurts out answers may blurt out excessively the first day. You need to be patient and allow for this. Eventually, the behavior will decrease. If the behavior becomes too intrusive for the rest of the class and is interfering with the class's ability to learn, another strategy should be tried.

4. Self-Monitoring/Preventative Cueing

Tape a chart on or inside the student's desk. Anytime the student is exhibiting the undesirable behavior, give the student some sort of cue (pointing the index finger at his or her desk) to indicate that the student should make a tally mark on the tally chart. The student eventually will begin to self-monitor the behavior and make the tally marks without direction from you. At the beginning of the day or week, establish the maximum number of tally marks which are acceptable. In order to do this, it is important to establish the baseline data. For example, let's assume that the target behavior is to decrease the out-of-seat behavior during independent work time and that it has been previously determined that the student is out of his seat an average of ten times per day. Therefore, you may decide to allow the student to receive nine tally marks the first couple of days before decreasing to eight. Start small; that way, you are more likely to see results quickly. Prior to starting the system, a reward system should be put into place. If the student meets his daily (hourly, weekly) goal, the student receives a reward. If the student does not meet the goal, the student does not receive the reward.

5. Token Economy/Response Cost

With this system, the student begins each day with a specific number of "points." Every time the student exhibits the undesirable behavior, a point is removed. For example, if a student starts the morning with ten points and is out of his seat five times during the day, five points (or 50%) remain at the end of the day. The reward is based on the number of points the student has at the end of the day. The criterion needs to be determined in advance. If the student does not have enough points, the response cost is that he or she will not have any points to "spend." Be sure that the goal is attainable, yet not too easy.

6. Behavior Contract

Write a contract with the student that states that he will raise his hand and wait to be called upon before responding during class. Positive reinforcements and rewards should be put into place when requirements listed on the contract are met. Consequences will follow if requirements are not met. The importance of a contract is to involve the student completely in the process. The student should have a copy of the contract to serve as a visual reminder at all times. (See example behavior contracts on pages 103-104.)

Section IV

Medications

Medications

To help many children show and feel success in school, doctors are prescribing medication to combat interfering factors. Children are being medicated for many different reasons including to assist with ADD/ADHD, anxiety, depression, emotional and behavioral problems, allergies, and seizures or convulsions. Listed and described below are **some** of the common medications that are being prescribed to school-aged children. A description of the medication is given as well as side effects that may result from these medications.

General Information about Medication

Each child and adolescent is different, and no two children or people have exactly the same combination of medical and psychological problems. When you are working with a child who is prescribed medication, it is a good idea to talk with the parents with regard to the reasons that this child is medicated. If the parents give permission, it would also be helpful and useful to talk with the doctor responsible for prescribing the medicine. It is important to administer the medication exactly as the doctor instructs. If a dosage of medication is forgotten while a child is in school, there may be special steps which will need to be followed. It is a good idea to ask the parents in advance what should occur if this were to happen. A school is not allowed, without parental permission, to stop or change the way of administering the medication. Many times, a medication is required to be taken with food, but lunchtime or snack time may change. If this is the case, be sure to notify the parent so that appropriate adjustments can be made.

If it appears to you, judging by the child's behavior in your classroom, that a medication is no longer being effective, this could mean that it is not being taken regularly. The student may be "cheeking" or hiding the medicine or forgetting to take it. Please inform the child's parents if you are noticing changes. Taking medication is a private matter and must be handled discreetly and confidentially. It is important to be sensitive to the student's feelings about taking the medicine.

Each medicine has a "generic" or chemical name. Just like laundry soap or paper towels, some medicines are sold by more than one company under different brand names. The same medicine may be available under a generic name and several brand names. It is important to know if the medication is a generic name or a brand name.

Anticonvulsants

What are anticonvulsants?
Anticonvulsants are usually used to treat seizures (convulsions). They are **sometimes** used to treat behavioral problems even if the student does not have seizures.

How can these medicines help?
Anticonvulsant medications can control seizure activity as well as reduce aggression, anger, and severe mood swings.

What are the common anticonvulsants used?
The chart below lists the most common anticonvulsant medications by the brand name and the generic names.

Brand Name	Generic Name
• Depakene or Depakote • Klonopin • Tegretol	• valproate or valproic acid • clonazapam • carbamazepine

How do these medicines work?
Anticonvulsants are thought to work by stabilizing a part of the brain cell or by increasing the concentration of certain chemicals in the brain.

What side effects might be seen from these medicines?
Any medication can have side effects, including an allergy to the medicine itself. Notify the student's parents and school nurse immediately if any of the following side effects appear or if you think that the medicine is causing any other problems.

Possible side effects of Tegretol (carbamazepine)

Common Side Effects	Less Common Side Effects	Serious/Rare Side Effects
• drowsiness • dizziness • unsteadiness • mild nausea (upset stomach) • vomiting • blurred or double vision • confusion • hostility • headache • severe water retention	• mood changes • behavioral changes • increased aggression • anxiety or nervousness • agitation or mania • hallucinations • impulsive/irritable behavior **Allergic Reactions** • hives • itching • rash	• severe behavior problems • loss of appetite • lung irritation • severe skin rash • worsening of seizures • affected liver function • unusual bruising or bleeding • swelling of legs of feet • yellowing of skin or eye

Possible side effects of Depakene/Depakote (valproic acid)

Common Side Effects	Less Common Side Effects	Serious/Rare Side Effects
• nausea • vomiting • indigestion • sleepiness • increased appetite • weight gain • depression • aggression • hyperactive behavior • increased irritability	• diarrhea • stomach cramps • constipation • hair loss • headache • drooping eyelids • double vision • loss of coordination • tremors	• yellowing of skin or eyes • unusual bruising or bleeding • mouth ulcers • skin rash • loss of appetite • swelling of legs or feet • sore throat • fever • severe behavioral problems

Possible side effects of Klonopin (clonazepam)

Common Side Effects	Less Common Side Effects	Serious/Rare Side Effects
• difficulty with balance • drowsiness/sleepiness • poor muscle control • behavioral changes	• irritability • excitement • increased anger/aggression • trouble sleeping • nightmares • memory loss	• uncontrollable behavior **If combined with alcohol:** • severe sleepiness • unconsciousness • death

What could happen if these medicines are stopped suddenly?

If carbamazepine or valproic acid is stopped suddenly, uncomfortable withdrawal symptoms will occur. If clonazepam is stopped suddenly, seizures could result if the child is being treated for seizures.

How long will these medicines be needed?

The length of time a person needs to take an anticonvulsant depends on what disorder is being treated. For example, with an impulse-control disorder, a person usually takes an anticonvulsant only until behavior therapy begins to work. Someone with bipolar disorder may need to take anticonvulsants for many years.

Antihistamines

What are antihistamines?

Antihistamines were developed to treat allergies. They are often used in children. They may be used to treat anxiety, insomnia, or the side effects of certain other medicines.

How can these medicines help?

Antihistamines may decrease nervousness. They work best for anxiety when used for a short time along with therapy. Occasionally they are used for longer periods of time to treat anxiety that remains after therapy is completed. They can also be used to help with insomnia when used for a short time along with a behavioral program.

What are the common antihistamines used?

The chart below lists the common brands of antihistamines and their generic names.

Brand Name	Generic Name
The following antihistamines will cause drowsiness:	
<ul><li>Atarax or Vistaril</li><li>Benadryl</li><li>Periactin</li></ul>	<ul><li>hydroxyzine</li><li>diphenhydramine</li><li>cyproheptadine</li></ul>
The following antihistamines are less likely to cause drowsiness:	
<ul><li>Allegra</li><li>Claritin</li><li>Clarinex</li><li>Zyrtec</li></ul>	<ul><li>fexofenadine</li><li>loratadine</li><li>desloratadine</li><li>cetirizine</li></ul>

How do these medicines work?

Antihistamines help reduce anxiety because of their sedative side effect. They make people a little sleepy so that they feel less nervous and tense.

What side effects might be seen from these medicines?

The most common side effect is sleepiness. If the medicine is causing drowsiness, it is very important that the child or adolescent not drive a car, ride a bicycle or motorcycle, or operate machinery. Decreased attention or learning will usually be obvious.

Possible side effects of antihistamines

Common Side Effects	Less Common Side Effects	Serious/Rare Side Effects
• decreased attention at school • drowsiness • dry mouth • loss of appetite • nausea • dizziness • excitation	• poor coordination • motor tics • unusual muscle movement • irritability • overactivity	• blurred/double vision • worsening of asthma • seizures • muscle stiffness • convulsions

What could happen if these medicines are stopped suddenly?

Stopping these medicines suddenly does not usually cause problems. Diarrhea or feeling ill may result.

How long will these medicines be needed?

When used to treat anxiety, antihistamines are usually prescribed for only a few weeks to allow the patient to be calm enough to learn new ways to cope with anxiety. When used to treat allergies, these medications are usually prescribed when seasonal allergies are most common (spring, early summer, and fall).

Antianxiety Medication: Benzodiazepines

What are antianxiety medications?

Several groups of medicines, often called sedatives or tranquilizers, are used to treat anxiety. The medicines most often used to treat anxiety or sleep problems are placed in two general groups: benzodiazepines and nonbenzodiazepines. The nonbenzodiazapines include Buspar, Antihistamines, and Beta-Blockers.

Benzodiazepines

How can these medicines help?

Antianxiety medicines decrease nervousness, fears, and excessive worrying. The benzodiazepines are particularly effective in decreasing the severe physical symptoms of anxiety disorders such as panic attacks and phobias. These medications are used for a short time when symptoms are very uncomfortable or frightening and make it difficult to do important things such as go to school.

Benzodiazepines can also be used for sleep problems such as night terrors or sleepwalking, which are dangerous or are making it impossible for other family members to get enough sleep

What are the common antianxiety medications: benzodiazepines?

The chart below lists the most common antianxiety medications by the brand name and the generic name.

Brand Name	Generic Name
The following medications are usually used to decrease anxiety, panic, or night terrors:	
<ul><li>Ativan</li><li>Klonopin</li><li>Librium</li><li>Valium</li><li>Xanax</li></ul>	<ul><li>lorazepam</li><li>clonazepam</li><li>chlordiazepoxide</li><li>diazepam</li><li>alprazolam</li></ul>
The following medications are usually used to treat sleep problems:	
<ul><li>Dalmane</li></ul>	<ul><li>flurazepam</li></ul>

How do these medicines work?

Antianxiety medicines work by calming the parts of the brain that are too excitable in anxious people. For example, they can help anxious people to be calm enough to learn and, with therapy, to understand and tolerate their worries or fears and even to overcome them.

What side effects might be seen from these medications?

The most common side effect is sleepiness. If the medicine is causing drowsiness, it is very important that the child or adolescent does not drive a car, ride a bicycle or motorcycle, or operate machinery. Benzodiazepines must not be combined with alcohol; severe sleepiness or even unconsciousness may result.

These medicines are usually safe when used for short periods of time as the doctor prescribes. Becoming dependent and addicted to benzodiazepines is possible, but that is not a great problem for patients who see their doctor regularly.

Sometimes antianxiety medicines seem to work backward, causing excitement, irritability, anger, aggression, trouble sleeping, nightmares, uncontrollable behavior, or memory loss. Call the parents right away if you see this happening.

Possible side effects of benzodiazepines

Common Side Effects	Less Common Side Effects	Serious/Rare Side Effects
• drowsiness • poor muscle control • behavioral changes • weakness • dizziness	• depression • disorientation • slurred speech • tremors • constipation • upset stomach/nausea	The medication can effect: • heart/stomach/intestines • urinary tract • blood • muscles • joints

What could happen if these medicines are stopped suddenly?
Many medicines cause problems if stopped suddenly. Problems are more likely to occur in patients taking high doses of benzodiazepines for two months or longer, but it is important to stop the medicine slowly even after a few weeks. Common withdrawal symptoms may include anxiety, irritability, shaking, sweating, aches and pains, muscle cramps, vomiting, and trouble sleeping. If large doses are stopped suddenly, seizures, hallucinations, or out-of-control behavior may result.

How long will these medicines be needed?
Benzodiazepines are usually prescribed for only a few weeks to allow the patient to become calm enough to learn new ways to cope with anxiety and to allow the nervous system to reset to a less excitable state. Each person is unique and some may need the medicines for months or years.

Buspar

How can this medicine help?
Antianxiety medicines decrease nervousness, fears, and excessive worrying. These drugs are used for a short time when symptoms are very uncomfortable or frightening, or when they make it hard to do important things such as go to school. Occasionally, they are used for longer periods to treat anxiety that remains after therapy is completed. Buspar is used to help reduce anxiety that may cause nervousness or behavior problems. It does not begin to help immediately. The full effect may not appear for 3-4 weeks.

Brand Name	Generic Name
• Buspar	• buspirone

What side effects might be seen from this medicine?

This medicine is usually very safe when used for short periods of time as the doctor prescribes. Sometimes antianxiety medicines seem to work backward, causing excitement, irritability, anger, aggression, trouble sleeping, nightmares, uncontrollable behavior, or memory loss. Contact parents immediately if this is noticed. Buspar may cause dizziness, nervousness, nausea, headache, restlessness, or trouble sleeping but does not cause dependence or sleepiness.

Common Side Effects	Less Common Side Effects	Serious/Rare Side Effects
• dizziness • nausea • headache • fatigue • nervousness/ excitement • light-headedness	• sleeplessness • chest pain / heart attack • rapid heartbeat • low blood pressure/fainting • depression • difficulty concentrating	The medication can affect: • heart/stomach/intestines • urinary tract • blood • muscles • joints

What could happen if this medicine is stopped suddenly?

Many medicines cause problems if stopped suddenly. Stopping slowly is a good idea to see if the anxiety recurs.

Beta-Blockers

What are Beta-Blockers?

Beta-blockers have been used primarily to treat high blood pressure and irregular heartbeat. Recently, however, these medications have also been used to treat emotional and behavior problems.

How can these medicines help?

Several studies of children and adolescents have shown that beta-blockers are effective in decreasing aggressive or violent behavior. These drugs may be particularly useful for patients who have developmental delays or autism. Beta-blockers may reduce the aggression and anger that sometimes follow brain injuries. These medicines may also reduce some symptoms of anxiety and help children and adolescents who have experienced very frightening events or have posttraumatic stress disorder.

What are the common beta-blockers used?

Brand Name	Generic Name
• Corgard • Inderal • Tenormin • Visken	• nadolol • propranolol • atenolol • pindolol

How do these medicines work?

When beta-blockers are prescribed for patients with anxiety, aggression, or other behavior problems, these medicines stop the effect of certain chemicals on nerves in the body and possibly in the brain that are causing the symptoms. For example, beta-blockers decrease the anxiety symptoms of shaking, sweating, and rapid heartbeat.

Possible side effects of beta-blockers

Common Side Effects	Less Common Side Effects	Serious/Rare Side Effects
• tingling, numbness, or pain in the fingers • tiredness or weakness • slow heartbeat • low blood pressure • dizziness (especially when standing up quickly.)	• nausea • trouble sleeping or nightmares • diarrhea • skin rash	• wheezing • sadness or irritability • hallucinations • muscle cramps

What happens if these medicines are stopped suddenly?

Stopping beta-blockers suddenly may cause a fast or irregular heartbeat, high blood pressure, and severe emotional problems. Beta-blockers should be discontinued gradually over a period of at least 2 weeks under a doctor's supervision.

How long will these medicines be needed?

The length of time the student will need to take beta-blockers depends on how well the medicine works for him or her and whether any side effects occur. Sometimes the student may need treatment lasting for several months.

Catapres (Clonidine) and Tenex (Guanfacine)

What are Catapres and Tenex?

Catapres (clonidine) and Tenex (guanfacine) were first used to treat high blood pressure. Now they are being used to treat symptoms of Tourette's disorder, chronic tics, and attention deficit/hyperactivity disorder (ADHD). They are occasionally used to treat aggression, posttraumatic stress disorder, anxiety, panic disorder, and bipolar (manic-depressive) disorder in children and adolescents. Both medicines are available as pills. Catapres also comes in a skin patch that releases medicine slowly for 5 days.

How can these medicines help?

Catapres and Tenex can decrease symptoms of hyperactivity, impulsivity, anxiety, irritability, temper tantrums, explosive anger, conduct problems, and tics. They can increase patience and frustration tolerance, as well as improve self-control and cooperation with adults. These medicines are sometimes used with Ritalin (methylphenidate) or Dexedrine (dextroamphetamine) for ADHD or with Haldol (haloperidol) or Orap (pimozide) for Tourette's disorder. The positive effects usually do not start for 2 weeks after a stable dose is reached. The full benefit may not be seen for 2-4 months.

How do these medicines work?

Catapres and Tenex work by decreasing the level of excitement in part of the brain. This effect helps people with tic disorders to stop moving or making noises when they do not want to. It also helps children with ADHD to slow down and think before acting. These medications are not sedatives or tranquilizers, even though they may seem that way because they can make the student sleepy when he or she first starts taking them.

Possible side effects of Catapres and Tenex

Common Side Effects	Less Common Side Effects	Serious/Rare Side Effects
• dizziness • drowsiness • headache • constipation or diarrhea • loss of appetite • fatigue • gas pains	• skin rash/itching • dry mouth • taste changes • blurred vision • leg cramps • bed-wetting • depression	• chest pain • shortness of breath • swelling of hands of feet • yellowing of eyes or skin • ringing in the ears

What could happen if these medicines are stopped suddenly?
If Catapres and Tenex are stopped suddenly, the following effects could result.

- Very high blood pressure, even if blood pressure was normal before starting meds
- Temporary worsening of behavior problems or tics
- Nervousness, anxiety
- Rapid or irregular heartbeat
- Chest pain
- Headache
- Stomach cramps, nausea, vomiting
- Trouble sleeping

Because of these effects, it is important not to stop these medications suddenly but to decrease them slowly as directed by the doctor. It is especially important not to miss doses of these medicines, because withdrawal symptoms or heart or blood pressure problems may occur. If the student takes a dose at school, it is essential not to let the prescription run out. It is especially important not to miss any Catapres doses if Ritalin is also being used.

How long will these medications be taken?
There is no way to know how long a person will need to take these medicines. The parents, the doctor, and the teacher will work together to determine what is right for each child. Sometimes the medicine may be needed for only a few years, but some people may need it longer.

Desyrel (Trazodone) and Serzone (Nefazodone)

What are Desyrel and Serzone?
Desyrel (trazodone) and Serzone (nefazodone) have been successfully used to treat depression in adults. Now these medicines are beginning to be used to treat emotional and behavior problems including depression, insomnia, and disruptive behavior disorders in children and adolescents.

How do these medicines help?
Desyrel and Serzone can decrease depression, irritability, and aggression. They can help a personto fall asleep at night.

How do these medicines work?
People with emotional and behavior problems may have low levels of a brain chemical called serotonin. Desyrel and Serzone are believed to help by increasing brain serotonin to more normal levels.

Possible side effects of Desyrel and Serzone

Common Side Effects	Less Common Side Effects	Serious/Rare Side Effects
• dizziness • drowsiness • dry mouth • headache • nausea	• light-headedness • fainting • blood in urine • shortness of breath • vomiting • irregular heartbeat	This medication can affect the: • liver • gastrointestinal tract • joints • skin

How long will these medicines be needed?

These medicines may not reach their full effect for several weeks. Therefore, the student may need to take this medicine for at least several months so that emotional or behavior problems do not recur.

Effexor (Venlafaxine)

What is Effexor?

Effexor (venlafaxine) has been used successfully to treat depression and anxiety in adults. Now this medication is being used to treat emotional and behavior problems, including anxiety, depression, and trouble with attention in children and adolescents.

How can Effexor help?

Effexor can decrease depression, irritability, and anxiety. It has been used to improve attention in children and adults.

How does this medicine work?

People with emotional and behavior problems may have unbalanced levels of certain chemicals in the brain. Effexor helps to restore the balance of these chemicals.

Possible side effects of Effexor

Common Side Effects	Less Common Side Effects	Serious/Rare Side Effects
• blurred vision • tiredness • dry mouth • dizziness • nervousness • nausea/vomiting • appetite loss/ weight gain	• dilated pupils • rapid heartbeat • anxiety • agitation • chills • yawning • lack of energy	• increased blood pressure • seizures (fits, convulsions)

What could happen if this medication is stopped suddenly?

No known serious medical withdrawal effects occur if Effexor is stopped suddenly, but there may be uncomfortable feelings.

How long will this medication be needed?

Effexor may take several weeks to reach its full effect. Therefore, the student may need to take the medication for at least several months so that the emotional or behavior problem does not recur.

Lithium

What is lithium?

Lithium is a naturally occurring salt that is available in several different forms, including lithium carbonate tablets (Lithotabs) or capsules (Eskalith or Lithonate), controlled-release capsules or tablets (Eskalith CR or Lithobid), and lithium citrate syrup.

How can these medicines help?

Lithium may be prescribed for bipolar (manic-depressive) disorder, certain types of depression, severe mood swings, and very serious aggression. It decreases mood swings, rage, and explosive aggression. It can reduce the frequency and severity of fighting or destroying property.

How does this medicine work?

Lithium acts by stabilizing nerve cells in the brain. This affects behavior in different ways depending on the problem that is being treated. For children with bipolar disorder, it works by leveling out the mood. For children with explosive aggression caused by rage, lithium works by "running down" the rage and decreasing the impulsivity. The student then has time to figure out more constructive ways to deal with his or her rage. Finally, for children and adolescents with depression whose symptoms have not responded to standard, single-drug therapy, lithium can make the antidepressant work better.

What side effects might be seen from lithium?

Whenever possible, lithium should be taken with food to decrease side effects. The side effects of lithium are increased if a person is dehydrated. If side effects appear, try giving the student one or two glasses of water. Soft drinks with caffeine may worsen side effects.

Side effects of lithium are directly related to the amount of drug in the bloodstream. It is very important to have the right amount of lithium in the body because too much of it may lead to unwanted effects. It is important that students are monitored closely by a doctor when taking this medication. **Overdosing with lithium may cause death.**

Possible side effects of lithium

Common Side Effects	Less Common Side Effects	Serious/Rare Side Effects
• fine hand tremor • thirst • excessive urination • mild nausea • discomfort	• diarrhea • vomiting • drowsiness • poor coordination • ringing/buzzing in ears • blurred vision	This medication can affect: • Muscles and nerves (blackouts/seizures/dizziness) • Stomach and intestines • Kidneys and urinary track • Skin • Thyroid function

What could happen if this medicine is stopped suddenly?

No adverse medical withdrawal effects occur right away if lithium is stopped suddenly. Some patients with bipolar disorder may become manic more often and be even more difficult to treat if lithium is stopped suddenly. If the student has been taking lithium for 6-8 weeks or longer, the dosage should be decreased gradually over 8-16 weeks before stopping in order to prevent this effect from happening.

How long will this medicine be needed?

For children and adolescents with bipolar disorder, is often prescribed for up to 2 years. Depending on how many times the student has had depression or mania, he or she may need to take the medicine indefinitely. Some patients do require lithium throughout their entire life to function normally. For rage, lithium must be continued for several months to years until the student, his or her family, and the doctor can find different ways to control the rage. Finally, for children and adolescents with severe depression who need lithium along with an antidepressant, lithium is usually needed for at least 5-6 months after the child's mood returns to normal. This is necessary to prevent the depression from recurring.

Neuroleptics

What are neuroleptics?

Neuroleptics are a group of medicines also called antipsychotic medicines. They used to be called major tranquilizers.

How can these medicines help?

Neuroleptics are used to treat psychosis such as schizophrenia, mania, or very severe depression. They may also be used for behavior problems after a head injury. They can reduce hallucinations and delusions and help the student be less upset and agitated. They can improve the ability to think clearly. Neuroleptics are also used to reduce motor and vocal tics and behavior problems in persons with Tourette's disorder. Sometimes they are used to reduce severe aggression or very serious behavior problems in young people with conduct disorder, mental impairments, or autism. These medicines are very powerful and are used to treat very serious problems or symptoms that do not respond to other medications. It is important to be patient. The positive effects of these medicines may not appear for 2-3 weeks.

What are the common neuroleptics used?

Brand Name	Generic Name
• Clozaril • Haldol • Loxitane • Mellaril • Moban • Navane • Orap • Prolixin • Risperdal • Stelazine • Thorazine • Trilafon • Zyprexa	• clozapine • haloperidol • loxapine • thioridazine • molindone • thiothixene • pimozide • fluphenazine • risperidone • trifluoperazine • chlorpromazine • perphenazine • olanzapine

How do these medication work?

One of the ways that the brain works is by creating substances called transmitters. Symptoms may be caused by too much or too little of these substances in the area of the brain that should receive the transmitters. Neuroleptics work on these transmitters and the areas of the brain that receive them so that the symptoms are reduced.

Possible side effects of neuroleptics

Common Side Effects	Less Common Side Effects	Serious/Rare Side Effects
• dry mouth • tiredness • constipation • mild trouble urinating • low blood pressure/fainting • fainting • headache • weight gain	• restlessness • nausea/upset stomach • sore throat • stiffness of tongue, jaw, neck, back, legs • increase breast size (in boys and girls)	• liver damage • extreme muscle stiffness • lack of movement • very high fever • mental confusion • inability to swallow • yellowing of eyes or skin

Most side effects diminish over time. Some can be reduced by decreasing the amount of medicine taken, by stopping the medicine, or by adding another medicine to combat the side effects. One side effect that may not go away is *tardive dyskinesia* (TD). Patients with tardive dyskinesia have involuntary movements of the body, especially the mouth and tongue. Jerky movements of the arms, legs, or body may occur. If you notice anything like this, be sure to inform the child's parents.

The following medicines may be used to treat the side effects of neuroleptics:

Brand Name	Generic Name
• Akineton	• biperiden
• Artane	• trihexyphenidyl
• Ativan	• lorazepam
• Benadryl	• diphenhydramine
• Catapres	• clonidine
• Cogentin	• benztropine mesylate
• Inderal	• propranolol
• Klonopin	• clonazepam
• Symmetrel	• amantadine

Selective Serotonin Reuptake Inhibitors (SSRIs)

What are SSRIs?

SSRIs have been used successfully to treat emotional and behavior problems, including depression, panic disorder, obsessive-compulsive disorder (OCD), bulimia, and posttraumatic stress disorder in adults. Now these medicines are being used to treat the same problems in children and adolescents.

What are the common SSRIs used?

Brand Name	Generic Name
• Celexa	• citalopram
• Luvox	• fluvoxamine
• Paxil	• paroxetine
• Prozac	• fluxetine
• Zoloft	• sertraline

How do these medicines work?

Serotonin is a chemical that is naturally found in the brain. Low levels of brain serotonin are associated with emotional and behavior problems. SSRIs help people by increasing the levels of brain serotonin to more normal levels.

Possible side effects of SSRIs

Common Side Effects	Less Common Side Effects	Serious/Rare Side Effects
• sweating • sleepiness • nausea • tremor • dry mouth • lack or loss of strength • headache • dizziness • restlessness	• weight loss or gain • hair loss • double vision • conjunctivitis (pink eye) • anemia • swelling • excitability or irritability • dizziness/fainting	• rash • hives • heatstroke • seizures

What could happen if these medicines are stopped suddenly?

No known serious medical withdrawal effects occur if SSRIs are stopped suddenly, but there may be uncomfortable feelings, such as trouble sleeping or even seeing things that are not there, especially in those who have used Paxil. Because Prozac is particularly long acting, an occasional missed dose is of less concern than with the other SSRIs.

How long will these medicines be needed?

SSRIs may take several weeks to reach their full effect. Therefore, the student may need to take the medicine for at least several months so that the emotional or behavior problem does not recur.

Stimulants

What are stimulants?

Stimulants are medicines that can improve attention span, decrease distractibility, increase ability to finish things, improve ability to follow directions, decrease hyperactivity, and improve ability to think before acting (decrease impulsivity). Handwriting and completion of schoolwork and homework can improve. Fighting and stubbornness in youngsters with attention-deficit/hyperactivity disorder can decrease. If stimulants do not work or cause problematic side effects, other medicines can be used.

What are the common stimulants used?

Brand Name	Generic Name
• Adderall	• amphetamine
• Concerta	• methylphenidate
• Cylert	• pemoline
• Desoxyn Gadumet Tablet	• methamphetamine
• Dexedrine	• dextroamphetamine
• Ritalin	• methylphenidate

How do these medicines work?

In children and adolescents who have ADHD, stimulant medicines stimulate parts of the brain that are not working as well as they should. An example would be the part that controls impulsive actions. These medicines are not tranquilizers or sedatives. They work in the same way in children and adults.

How long do these medicines last?

The effect of Ritalin and Dexedrine usually lasts for three to four hours. Thus, symptoms may return in the late morning or late in the day. The longer-acting medicines, such as Ritalin Sustained-Release (SR) tablets, Dexedrine Spansule capsules, Cylert tablets, and Desoxyn Gradume tablets have effects that will last as long as six to eight hours.

What if the student misses a dose?

The school health center will monitor the student. If the student misses a dose, the medication may be taken within one hour and the normal schedule resumed. If the student completely misses the scheduled dose, the SSRI should not be doubled during the next dosage.

Possible side effects of stimulants

Common Side Effects	Less Common Side Effects	Serious/Rare Side Effects
• loss of appetite • trouble sleeping • stomach pain • dizziness • rapid heartbeat • constipation/cramps • dry mouth • irritability, crankiness • emotional sensitivity	• rebound (hyperactivity or intensity of mood as medicine is wearing off) • slowing of growth (growth usually catches up if medicine is stopped or dose is decreased) • nervous habits • picking at skin / stuttering	• rash • hives • heatstroke • seizures

What happens if these medicines are stopped suddenly?

No medical withdrawal effects occur if stimulants are stopped suddenly. A few young people may experience irritability, trouble sleeping, or increased hyperactivity for a day or two if they have been taking medicine every day for a long time, especially at high doses. It may be better to decrease the medicine slowly over a week or so.

How long will these medicines be needed?

There is no way to know for certain how long a person will need to take these medicines. The parents, doctors, and teachers will work together to determine what is right for each young person. Sometimes the medicine is needed for only a few years, but some people may need to take medicine even as adults.

Other things to know about these medicines:

Stimulants do not cause illegal drug use or addiction. However, because the patient or other people may abuse these medicines, adult supervision is important. Some young people take the medicine three or four times a day, every day. Others need to take it only twice a day and only on school days.

It is important for the student not to chew Ritalin-SR tablets or Dexedrine Spansule capsules because this releases too much medicine all at once.

Strattera (atomoxetine)

What is Strattera (atomoxetine)?

Strattera (atomoxetine) is a selective norepinephrine reuptake inhibitor used to treat attention deficit hyperactivity disorders (ADHD).

How does it work?

Strattera works by helping to restore the balance of certain natural chemicals in the brain.

How is this medicine different from the others used to treat ADHD?

Strattera is not a stimulant like the other common medications used to treat ADHD.

Possible side effects of Strattera

Common Side Effects	Less Common Side Effects	Serious/Rare Side Effects
• upset stomach • nausea • constipation • fatigue • loss of appetite • dry mouth	• vomiting • trouble sleeping • mood changes • difficulty urinating • dizziness	• rapid heartbeat • blurred vision • weight loss • severe headache • rash/itching • trouble breathing

What could happen if this medicine is stopped suddenly?

No known medical withdrawal effects occur if Strattera is stopped suddenly, but there may be some uncomfortable feelings. Some people may experience irritability, trouble sleeping, or increased hyperactivity.

How long will this medication be needed?

There is no way to know for certain how long a person will need to take this medication. Parents, doctors, and teachers should work together to determine what is right for each young person. Sometimes the medicine is needed for only a few years, but some people may need to take this medicine even as an adult.

What if a dose is missed?

If a dose is missed it should be taken as soon as possible. If it is almost time for the next dose, skip the missed dose and return to the regular dosing schedule. Do not double up the dosage.

Tricyclic Antidepressants

What are tryicyclic antidepressants?

Tricyclic antidepressants were first used to treat depression but are now also used to treat enuresis (bed wetting), attention-deficit hyperactivity disorder, school phobia, separation anxiety, panic disorder, obsessive-compulsive disorder (OCD), some sleep disorders (such as night terrors,) and trichotillomania (compulsive pulling out of one's hair) in children and adolescents.

How can these medicines help?

Tricyclic antidepressants can decrease depression, anxiety, panic, obsessions and compulsions, bed-wetting, night terrors or sleepwalking, and symptoms of ADHD. Each medicine in this group is better for some symptoms than for others. When treating enuresis, the medicine works right away. When treating depression, the medicine may take several weeks to work.

What are the common tricyclic antidepressants used?

Brand Name	Generic Name
• Anafranil • Elavilor Endep • Norpramin or Petofrane • Pamelor or Aventyl • Tofranil	• clomipramine • amitriptyline • desipramine • nortriptyline • impramine

How do these medicines work?

When tricyclic antidepressants are prescribed for people with depression, these medicines affect the natural substances that are needed for certain parts of the brain to work more normally. For instance, the parts of the brain that regulate concentration, motivation, or mood will work better with help from these medicines.

Possible side effects of tricyclic antidepressants

Common Side Effects	Less Common Side Effects	Serious/Rare Side Effects
• dry mouth • constipation • blurred vision • dizziness • weight gain • loss of appetite/weight loss • sleepiness • irritability	• anxiety • restlessness • poor coordination • high or low blood pressure • upset stomach • diarrhea • enlargement of breasts (both male and female).	• seizures • irregular heartbeat • fainting • hallucinations • inability to urinate • confusion • severe changes in behavior • rash/ itching

What could happen if these medicines are stopped suddenly?

Stopping the medicine or skipping a dose is not dangerous but can be very uncomfortable. It may feel like coming down with the flu (having a headache, muscle aches, stomach ache, and upset stomach). Behavior problems, sadness, nervousness, or trouble sleeping may occur. If these feelings appear daily, the medicine may need to be given more often during each day.

How long will these medicines be needed?

There is no way to know for certain how long a person will need to take these medicines. The parents, doctors, and teachers will work together to determine what is right for each child.

Wellbutrin (Bupropion)

What is Wellbutrin (bupropion)?

Wellbutrin (bupropion) has been used successfully to treat depression in adults. Now this medicine is beginning to be used to treat emotional and behavior problems, including depression, attention-deficit hyperactivity disorder, and conduct problems in children and adolescents.

How can this medicine help?

Wellbutrin can decrease depression, impulsive behavior, and aggression.

How does this medicine work?

Wellbutrin helps people by normalizing the levels of certain chemicals that are naturally found in the brain.

Possible side effects of Wellbutrin (bupropion)

Common Side Effects	Less Common Side Effects	Serious/Rare Side Effects
• dry mouth • dizziness • rapid heartbeat • headache • excessive sweating • nausea • appetite loss • weight changes • sleeplessness	• upset stomach • increased appetite • muscle spasms • trouble sleeping • swelling around the mouth	• abnormal heart rhythms • blood pressure changes • heart palpitations • loss of concentration • rash/itching • seizures • vomiting • unusual excitement • rapid speech

What could happen if this medicine is stopped suddenly?

No known medical withdrawal effects occur if Wellbutrin is stopped suddenly. Some people may get a headache as the medicine wears off. If the medicine is stopped, the original problems may recur. Parents should consult the doctor before stopping the medicine with their child.

How long will this medicine be needed?

Wellbutrin may take several weeks to reach its full effect. Therefore, the student may need to take the medicine for at least several months so that the emotional or behavior problem does not recur.

Other information about this medicine:

It can be very dangerous to take Wellbutrin at the same time as, or even within several weeks of, taking another type of medicine called a monomania oxides inhibitor.

Section V

Teacher Resources

Attention Deficit Disorder (ADD)
Attention Deficit Hyperactivity Disorder (ADHD)

Websites

www.chadd.org
> Children and Adults with Attention Deficit/Hyperactivity Disorder (CHADD)

www.cdipage.com
> Attention Deficit Hyperactivity Disorder, ADD

www.add.org
> National Attention Deficit Disorder Association (ADDA)

http://groups.msn.com/ADDedSupport
> ADD/ADHD online support group

Resource Books

ADD/ADHD Behavior Change Resource Kit: Ready-to-Use Strategies and Activities for Helping Children with Attention Deficit Disorder
Flick, Grad. 1998, 391 pp. Jossey-Bass
For teachers, counselors, and parents, this comprehensive resource is filled with up-to-date information and practical strategies to help kids with ADD and ADHD learn to control and change their behavior

Attention Without Tension: A Teacher's Handbook on Attention Disorders
Copeland, Edna D & Love, Valerie L. 1995, 178 pp. 2nd Ed. Specialty Press, Incorporated.
Practical information and ideas to use in the class when teaching children with ADD and ADHD.

Coping with ADD/ADHD
Morrison, Jaydene, 1997, 93pp. Hazelden Information and Educational Services.
Easy-to-understand information which helps children with ADD/ADHD to understand the disorder and provides practical assistance in how to cope with the effects of ADD/ADHD.

Everything You Need to Know about ADD/ADHD.
Beal, Eileen. 1998, 64 pp. The Rosen Publishing Group, Incorporated.
Defines ADD and ADHD and discusses what can be done to treat the conditions, including medication, behavior modification, and counseling

How to Reach and Teach ADD/ADHD Children- K-8
Rief, Sandra, 2005 John Wiley

This fully updated second edition provides management techniques that promote on-task behavior along with strategies to help with LA, math, writing and multi-sensory instruction strategies that maintain student attention and keep students actively involved with learning.

Pants with Pockets and Other Tips on Managing an ADD/ADHD Child.
Matos, Candi & Matos, Chris. 1999, 138 pp. 2nd Ed. The Herbal Way.

Provides practical strategies and tips on effectively handling children with ADD and ADHD.

Putting on the Brakes: Young People's Guide to Understanding Attention Deficit Disorder
Quinn, Patricia O.; Stern, Judith M. 2001, 80 pp. Revised Edition. American Psychological Association.

This book is a guide for 8-13 year olds with attention deficit disorder, written from a pediatric and educational perspective. The publications addresses questions and needs, the latest advances in treatment programs and medications to help children manage their ADD

Children's Picture Books

Eddie Enough!
Zimmett, Debbie. 2001, 48 pp. Woodbine House.

Third-grader Eddie Minetti is described as a human whirlwind. He is always getting into trouble at school until his ADHD is diagnosed and treated

Eukee, the Jumpy, Jumpy Elephant
Corman, Clifford & Trevino, Esther. 1995, 22 pp. Specialty Press, Incorporated.

This is the story of a young elephant's struggle with attention deficit disorder. Eukee gets into trouble at home and school because he can't sit still and follow directions. He gets help at home and from a special doctor and learns ways to succeed.

Shelley: The Hyperactive Turtle
Moss, Deborah M. 1989, 19 pp. Woodbine House.

After his mother takes him to the doctor, Shelley the turtle begins to understand why he feels so jumpy and wiggly inside that he can't sit still

Sparky's Excellent Misadventures: My A.D.D. Journal
Carpenter, Phyllis, Ford, Marti, and Horjus, Peter (ill.), 2000, 32 pp. Magination.

Sparky is a boy with ADD, which makes his life very exciting! With a little help from his family and school, and by writing about his ups and downs in his journal, he is figuring out how to "manage his wiggles and keep all of the giggles." Told in a first-person diary format, Sparky's week-in-the-life tale is optimistic and fun, and includes many valuable insights and ideas that can help kids with ADD and ADHD gain more control of their lives.

Anxiety

Websites

www.adaa.org
> ADAA - Anxiety Disorders Association of America

www.anxietypanic.com
> Anxiety/Panic Attack Resource Site

www.childhoodanxietynetwork.org
> Childhood anxiety network homepage

www.childanxiety.net
> User-friendly information about child anxiety

Resource Books

Anxiety Disorders in Children and Adolescents
March, John S. 1995, 448 pp. Guilford Publications, Inc.
A collection of papers about anxiety disorders in children and adolescents. This book provides information of the recognition and treatment of childhood-onset anxiety syndromes.

A Handbook of Childhood Anxiety Management
Dwivedi, Kedar N (ed.) & Varma, Ved (ed). 1997, 252 pp, Ashgate Publishing Co.
This book addresses the causes, nature, and distribution of anxiety problems in children and offers various approaches to treatment. It is aimed at assisting professionals in offering skillful help to children.

Test Anxiety & What You Can Do About It
Casbarro, J 2004 National Professional Resources
Testing often creates anxiety, which in turn often lowers the students' performance. Help to prepare your students by identifying the cause of the anxiety and learn techniques to use during pre-testing, test-in-progress, and post-testing phases which will help reduce the physical/emotional symptoms, increase concentration, and attention which will result in better test performance.

Your Anxious Child: How Parents and Teachers Can Relieve Anxiety in Children
Dacey, John S. 2001, 256 pp. John Wiley and Sons, Inc.
This book empowers parents and teachers to teach children essential coping skills for dealing with anxiety in engaging, creative ways. Through dozens of activities, children will learn how to alleviate stress, build courage and trust, and become innovative problem solvers.

Autism

Websites

www.healthieryou.com/autism.html
Autism Fact Sheet

www.unc.edu/depts/teacch
Autism Primer - Twenty Questions

www.autism.org
Center for the Study of Autism

www.autism.com
Autism Research Institute

www.autism-pdd.net
Support for Autism Spectrum Disorder

Resource Books

Activity Schedules for Children with Autism
McClannahan, Lynn, Krantz, Patricia J. 1999, 117 pp. Woodbine House.
This book is a great resource for parents and teachers of children with autism as it provides detailed explanations and examples of activity schedules. It demonstrates how effectively activity schedules can foster greater independence and social awareness in the daily lives of children with autism

Autism: Information and Resources for Parents, Families and Professionals
Simpson, Richard L., Zionts, Paul. 1992, 172 pp. Pro-Ed.
This book is set up in a question-answer format for parents and families, to answer many of the most commonly asked questions about autism

Autism Spectrum Disorders
Simpson, R. 2005, 336 pp. Paul Brookes Publishing Co.
Autism Spectrum Disorders (ASD) was developed to respond directly to the difficulty school professionals and families face in selecting an applying appropriate interventions and treatments for the children in their care.

Autism: The Facts
Baron-Cohen, Simon; Bolton, Patrick. 1993, 113 pp. Oxford University Press, Incorporated.
A book for parents and educators explaining what is known about autism from the scientific point of view.

Children with Autism – A Parent's Guide (Birth – age 7)
Powers, M., 2000, 427 pp. Woodbine House
Revised and updated this publication covers a multitude of special concerns including daily and family life, early intervention, education programs, legal rights and more.

Demystifying Autism Spectrum Disorders – A Guide to Diagnosis for Parents and Professionals Bruey, Caroly Thorwarth, 2004, 241 pp. Woodbine House
This guide for lay readers-parents, educators, and caregivers- describes the five types of autism that fall under the ASD umbrella, spells out the distinctions among them, demystifies the technical jargon, and provides and overview of Treatment.

Do-Watch-Listen Say Social and Communication Intervention for Children with Autism Quill, K., 540 pp. Paul H Brookes Publishing Company
This comprehensive intervention guide and accompanying activities are easily adapted to develop a curriculum for both children who are verbal and those who use augmentative and alternate communication. This user-friendly resource provides the methods needed to build social and communication skills in children with autism (PreK – 8th grade).

Facing Autism: Giving Parents Reasons for Hope and Guidance for Help
Hamilton, Lynn M., & Rimland, Bernard. 2000, 266 pp. Waterbrook Press.
Now parents of autistic children can find the hope and practical guidance they need. Perhaps one of the most devastating things parents can learn is that their child has been diagnosed with autism. A multifaceted disorder, autism has long baffled parents and professionals alike. At one time, doctors gave parents virtually no hope for combating the disorder. But in recent years, new treatments and therapies have demonstrated that improvement is possible.

Reaching Out, Joining In
Weiss, Mary Jane, Harris, Sandra L. 2001, 150 pp. Woodbine House.
An excellent guide for parents and teachers to utilize when assisting students with autism in becoming better socially adjusted at home and at school

Right from the Start
Harris, Sandra L., Weiss, Mary Jane. 1998, 138 pp. Woodbine House.
This book is an informative guide for both parents and teachers of children with autism. It provides behavioral intervention ideas to utilize with young children with autism.

The Hidden Child
Simons, Jeanne, Oishi, Sabine. 1987, 286 pp. Woodbine House.
This guidebook is written for teachers and therapists. It utilizes the Linwood Method for reaching the autistic child. The Linwood Method provides an informative look at autism as well as a uniquely successful treatment program for the autistic child.

The World of the Autistic Child: Understanding and Treating Autistic Spectrum Disorders Siegel, Bryna. 1996, 368 pp. Oxford University Press.
This is a complete and comprehensive study written for parents of autistic children and for teachers, child specialists, and other professionals who care for them. It provides help and hope not only for the autistic child, but also for their families and other caregivers who must come to grips with their own grief, confusion, and self-doubt following a diagnosis of autism or other related disorder.

"You're Going to Love this Kid!" Teaching Students with Autism in the Inclusive Classroom (K-12)
Kluth, P, 2004 Paul Brookes Publishing Co.
This is a strategy-filled guidebook for including students with autism in both primary and secondary school classrooms. The publication demonstrates how educators can adapt their own classrooms to support student participation, school routines, social activities and more.

Children's Picture Books

Andy and His Yellow Frisbee
Thompson, Mary. 1996, 20 pp. Woodbine House.
This book tells the story of a new girl at school who tries to befriend Andy, an autistic boy, who spends every recess by himself.

Mori's Story: A Book About a Boy with Autism
Gartenberg, Zachary and Gay, Jerry (ill.) 1998, 40 pp. The Lerner Publishing Group.
A young boy discusses his home life and schooling with his autistic brother, Mori. He discusses how his family learned that Mori was autistic, the kinds of treatment Mori receives, and how it affects all of their lives.

My Brother Sammy
Edwards, Becky. 1999, 32 pp. Millbrook Press.
This book's narrator longs for a brother who can talk to him, build towers with him, and join his friends at play. His autistic brother Sammy mimics his speech, knocks down his building blocks, and lies alone on the grass staring at the leaves on trees. As the older boy tries doing and seeing things Sammy's way, a special relationship develops between them.

Russell is Extra Special: A Book about Autism in Children
Amenta, Charles A. III. 1992, 15 pp American Psychological Association.
This book was written to help children learn about autism. The author is the father of a child with autism as well as a physician. Parents, teachers, and other professionals will find this book very helpful

Bi-Polar Disorder (Manic Depression)

Websites

www.psycom.net/depression.central.bipolar.html
   Bipolar Disorder - Manic Depression

www.bipolar.com
   Bipolar Website

Resource Books

Bipolar Disorder in Childhood and Early Adolescence
Geller, Barbara (ed.) and Delbellow, Melissa P., (ed). 2003, 342 pp. Guildford Press
This book provides and overview of the theory, research, and knowledge in childhood-onset bipolar illness. It addresses such topics as epidemiology, diagnosis and assessment, and the life course of the disorder. It describes ways in which the bipolar illness presents itself differently in children than in adults.

Survival Strategies for Parenting Children with Bipolar Disorder: Innovative Parenting and Counseling Techniques for Helping Children with Bipolar Disorder and the Conditions That May Occur with It
Lynn, George T. 2000, 240 pp. Jessica Kingsley Publishing
Up until five years ago, the professional community did not think that bipolar disorder occurred in children. Now, as it is being increasingly diagnosed, this book offers clear, practical advice on recognizing the symptoms, understanding medication, and accessing the necessary support at school as well as managing the day-to-day challenges of parenting a child with bipolar disorder.

The Bipolar Child: The Definitive and Reassuring Guide to Childhood's Most Misunderstood Disorder, Vol. 1
Papolos, Demitri F., Papolos, Janice. 1999, 398 pp. Broadway Books
This book is about early-onset bipolar disorder. Bipolar disorder was once thought to be rare in children; however, researchers are now discovering that not only can bipolar disorder begin very early in life, but it is also much more common than ever imagined. This book asks, "Why is this illness often misdiagnosed or overlooked?"

Bronchopulmonary Dysplasia

Websites

www.mesothelioma-asbestosis.info/Lung-Diseases/Bronchopulmonary-Dysplasia-BPD
Bronchopulmonary Dysplasia (BPD) – Causes, Symptoms, Diagnosis, Treatment, Cures and Remedies

www.depts.washington.edu/growing/assess/BPD
Assuring care for preterm infants

Resource Book

The Official Patients Sourcebook on Bronchopulmonary Dysplasia
Parker, James N. (ed), Parker, Philip M. (ed). 2002, 204 pp. Icon Health Publications
This book has been created for parents who have decided to make education and research an integral part of the treatment process. It provides resources for where to look for information covering virtually all topics related to bronchopulmonary dysplasia (also perinatal bronchopulmonary dysplasia) from the essentials to the most advanced areas of research.

Cerebral Palsy

Websites

www.irsc.org/cerebral.htm
   Cerebral Palsy (CP)

www.nlm.nih.gov/medlineplus/cerebralpalsy.html
   Medline plus health information

Resource Books

Children with Cerebral Palsy: A Parent's Guide
Geralis, Elaine. 1998, 424 pp. 2nd Ed. Woodbine House.
This book is a complete and compassionate guide to everything parents need to know about raising their child with cerebral palsy and meeting their varied medical, therapeutic, and educational needs.

Coping with Cerebral Palsy: Answers to Questions Parents Often Ask
Schleichkorn, Jay. 1996, 252 pp. 2nd Ed. Pro-Ed International Publisher.
In this book, questions most frequently asked by parents are answered. Information is obtained by searching the literature, talking with professional personnel, meeting with parents, and talking to adults with cerebral palsy.

Everything You Need to Know about Cerebral Palsy
Pincus, Dion. 1999, 64 pp. Rosen Publishing Group.
This book begins with a description of the characteristics or symptoms that constitute the condition or physical disability.   It also discusses the causes, both known and speculated, medical treatments, schooling, and the family life of individuals. The language in this book is simple, with medical terms explained both in the text and in the glossary

My Perfect Son has Cerebral Palsy: A Mother's Guide of Helpful Hints
Kennedy, Marie A. 2001, 108 pp. 1st Books Library.
Marie Kennedy's story of her son's coping with cerebral palsy is one of hope, strength, love, encouragement, and courage. This book provides useful information for anyone, regardless of whether their immediate family has been touched by cerebral palsy or not. It is written in a simple style to make it easy for the reader to get the most out of it in the least amount of time

Children's Picture Books

Howie Helps Himself
Fassler, Joan, Lasker, Joe (ill.) 1991, 29 pp. Albert Whitman Publishing
Howie, a boy with cerebral palsy, enjoys life and loves his family; however, he wants more than anything to be able to move his wheelchair himself.

I'm the Big Sister Now
Emmert, Michelle., Owens, Gail (ill). 1991, 32 pp. Albert Whitman Publishing.
Nine-year-old Michelle describes the joys, difficulties, and special situations involved in living with her older sister Amy, who was born severely disabled with cerebral palsy

Taking Cerebral Palsy to School
Anderson, Elizabeth Mary, Gosselin, Kim (ed) & Dineen, Tom (ill.) 2000, 32pp. JayJo Books, L L C.
This book is written from the perspective of a child with CP. It answers many of the questions his classmates have, but are too scared to ask. Children, teachers, school nurses, parents, and caregivers will all learn about CP.

Nathan's Wish: A Story About Cerebral Palsy
Lears, L., Schuett, Stacy. 2005 Albert Whitman & Co
Nathan lives next door to Miss Sandy, a raptor rehabilitator. She's very busy taking care of injured birds of prey, like owls and hawks. Nathan wishes he could help Miss Sandy with some of her chores, but he is confined to his wheelchair because of cerebral palsy. Then Fire, an owl with a broken wing, comes to Miss Sandy. Fire is desperate to fly and Nathan can't wait for Fire to get her wish. Nathan desperately searches for a way to help Fire, not realizing that what he finds will help transform his life as well.

Rolling Along: The Story of Taylor and His Wheelchair
Heelan, Jamee Riggio, Simmonds, Nicola (Ill.) 2000 Albert Whitman & Co
This book for K-3 students provides a glimpse into the life of a young boy with cerebral palsy. Taylor describes his condition, aspects of his daily activities at home and at school, and his desire for independence. At times, Taylor's frustrations come through, as when the illustrator shows him in his wheelchair facing a rather high set of stairs. However, in the end, the message is that he enjoys the same activities as his twin (and other children).

Chronic Fatigue Syndrome

Websites

www.cdc.gov/ncidod/diseases/cfs/index.htm
Chronic Fatigue Syndrome Home Page

www.immunesupport.com
Chronic Fatigue Syndrome and Fibromyalgia Resource

www.aacfs.org
The American Association for Chronic Fatigue Syndrome - AACFS

Resource Books

A Parent's Guide to CFIDS: How to Be an Advocate for your Child with Chronic Fatigue Immune Dysfunction
Bell, David S., Robinson, Mary Z., Robinson, Tom, Floyd, Bonnie. 1999, 143 pp. Haworth
This book assists parents and others in understanding chronic fatigue immune dysfunction syndrome (CFIDS) in children. The book combines medical, parental, and personal experiences designed to minimize the negative social and educational effects on children with CFIDS, and shows how to help affected children overcome the major academic and social challenges of CFIDS.

Chronic Fatigue Syndrome: The Hidden Epidemic
Stoff, Jesse A; Pellegrino, Charles R.; & Geiss, Tony. 1992, 384 pp. Harper Trade.
This book explains the difficult-to-diagnose and impossible-to-"cure" chronic fatigue syndrome. It is considered a breakthrough guide for anyone sick and tired of feeling sick and tired.

Running on Empty: The Complete Guide to Chronic Fatigue Syndrome
Berne, Katrina H. 1995, 315 pp. (2nd ed.) Hunter House, Incorporated.
This book offers a definition of CFS as well as the history, symptoms, and effects this has on patients' lives. The book discusses options for treatment as well as ways to cope with CFS.

Conduct Disorders

Websites

www.klis.com/chandler/pamphlet/oddcd/oddcdpamphlet.htm
Oppositional Defiant Disorder (ODD) and Conduct Disorder (CD) in Children and Adolescents.

www.mentalhealth.com/dis/p20-ch02.html
Conduct Disorder

www.athealth.com/Practitioner/Newsletter/FPN_3_7.html
Disruptive Behavior Disorders

www.conductdisorders.com
A Conduct Disorders support group

Resource Books

Complete Early Childhood Behavior Management Guide
Watkins, Kathleen P. & Durant, Lucius. 1997, 192 pp. The Center for Applied Research in Education.
This guide provides insight and tools to obtain the best possible behavior from young children, as well as effective, child-tested strategies for resolving problem behaviors when they occur.

Conduct Disorders in Childhood and Adolescence, Vol. 9
Kazdin, Alan E. 1995, 200 pp (2nd ed) Sage Publications, Incorporated.
This book describes the nature of conduct disorder and what is now known based on recent research and clinical work. Attention is also given to key risk factors of conduct disorders, treatments of conduct disorders, and prevention of conduct disorders.

Helping Children with Aggression and Conduct Problems: Best Practices for Intervention Watkins, Kathleen P., Durant, Lucius. 1997, 192 pp. The Center for Applied Research
The authors attempt to define the nature of the problem of aggressive children and present contemporary thinking about theories that account for the development and maintenance of patterns of antisocial behavior. They also address intervention strategies in school and public settings.

Preventing Childhood Disorders, Substance Abuse, and Delinquency
Peters, Ray D. & McMahon, Robert J. (Ed) 1996, 364 pp. Sage Publications Incorporated.
This book presents the results of recent research on early-intervention programs with children from birth to adolescence. Among them are social-skills training for children with conduct disorder, anger-coping group work for aggressive children, parent-training programs, and programs for high-risk children.

The Defiant Child: A Parent's Guide to Oppositional Defiant Disorder
Riley, Douglas, A. 1997, 224 pp. Taylor Publishing
This easy-to-read publication attempts to give a tough, no-nonsense approach for parents to remain in control when the child is displaying negative, angry, and hostile behavior towards adults. Actual stories and real cases are used to describe behavior plans and options.

Cystic Fibrosis

Websites

www.cff.org
Cystic Fibrosis Foundation

www.cfri.org
Cystic Fibrosis Research, Inc. (CFRI)

www.cysticfibrosis.com
Living with Cystic Fibrosis

Resource Books

A Parent's Guide to Cystic Fibrosis
Shapiro, P. L. & Heussner, Ralph C. 1990, 120 pp. University of Minnesota Press.
A clear and comprehensive guide written to help parents and professionals understand the nature, cause and treatment of cystic Fibrosis. The text is filled with comments from parents and patients and includes a chapter devoted to family life.

Understanding Cystic Fibrosis
Hopkins, Karen. 1998, 128 pp. University Press of Mississippi.
Cystic fibrosis (CF) is the most common genetic disorder in the white population. Understanding CF charts the progress that has been made in identifying the cause of CF

Children's Picture Books

Taking Cystic Fibrosis to School
Henry, Cynthia S., Gosselin, Kim (ed) & Dineen, Tom (ill.) 2000, 32 pp. Jayjo Books, L L C.
This book is written from the perspective of a child with cystic fibrosis to explain and educate her classmates about her condition. This book is designed to help kids, families, teachers, school nurses and caregivers to better understand cystic fibrosis

Depression

Websites

www.nami.org/ContentGroups/Helpline1/Facts_About_Childhood_Depression.htm
Facts about childhood depression

www.bestsitez.com/depression
Causes, varieties, symptoms and solutions to depression, mailing list, depression discussion board, online counselors and more.

www.hoptechno.com/book34.htm
Depression: Define It. Defeat It.

www.childcare.org/parents/article-childhood-depression.htm
Facts for parents about childhood depression

Resource Books

The Childhood Depression Sourcebook
Miller, Jeffry A. 1999, 228 pp. McGraw-Hill Contemporary Books.
This book provides resources for everything you need to know about diagnosing the symptoms of childhood depression, problems that may occur due to depression (such as anxiety, ADD/ADHD, and substance abuse), and treatment methods, including psychotherapy

Growing Up Sad: Childhood Depression and Its Treatment
Cytryn, Leon & McKnew, Donald H. 1998, 216 pp. Norton.
This book presents information on the advances in diagnosis and treatment of childhood depression. Specific characteristics of depression, environmental and biological causes, and treatments are discussed.

Help Me, I'm Sad
Fassler, David G., Dumas, Lynne S. 1998, 224 pp. Penguin USA.
A reassuring guide for parents of adolescents whose lives are darkened by depression. This book helps to recognize, treat, and prevent childhood and adolescent depression.

My Depression: A Picture Book
Swados, Elizabeth. 2005, 176 pp. Hyperion
Elizabeth Swados, candidly presents this zingy cartoon memoir in which she chronicles her struggles with severe depression. In expressively scribbled drawings and scrawled, to-the point commentary, Swados charts the course her depression takes and itemizes the symptoms, which range from insulting her friends to failing to get out of bed. This seemingly simple tale conveys a wealth of helpful information and dispels the gloom a bit by making readers laugh.

Down Syndrome

Websites

www.nas.com/downsyn
   Family Empowerment Network: A resource for families of children with DS

www.dsrf.org
   Down Syndrome Foundation

www.nads.org
   National Association for Down Syndrome

Resource Books

Down Syndrome: The Facts
Selikowitz, Mark. 1990, 205 pp. Oxford University Press, Incorporated.
This book has been written for parents who have a child with Down syndrome. It would also be of interest to friends, teachers, and therapists who come into contact with children with Down syndrome.

Down Syndrome: Living and Learning in the Community
Nadel, Lynn (ed)., Rosenthal, Donna (ed). 1995, 297 pp. John Wiley and Sons, Incorporated.
This book provides information and advice about Down syndrome including an overview of the latest medical advances and information about the programs and services now available.

**Teaching Math to People with Down Syndrome and Other Hands-On Learners –
Book 1 Basic Survival Skills**
Horstmeier, DeAnna, 2004, 408 pp. Woodbine House
Educators and parents can use this guide to teach meaningful math to students with and without disabilities who struggle with understanding computation, number concepts, and when and how to use these skills. A key feature of this method is the early introduction of the calculator which allows students to progress without memorizing math facts. This book may be used to help students learn the critical math survival skills needed to live independently. Book 1 cover introductory math skills typically taught in preschool or elementary school but which many older students still need help and support.

Teaching Reading to Children with Down Syndrome
Oelwein, P, 1995, 371 pp. Woodbine House
This nationally known reading program ensures success by presenting lessons which are both imaginative and functional and can be tailored to meet the needs of each student.
The book includes 100 pages of reproducible materials to supplement the program. This program will not only help students with DS but many struggling readers.

Early Communication Skills for Children with Down Syndrome – A Guide for Parents and Professionals.
Kumin, Libby. 2003, 368 pp. Woodbine House
This publication includes the latest research on DS and communication. The book focuses on speech and language development from birth through 3 word phrases, usually beginning at age 4 or 5. It fully covers speech and language assessment; what to expect in the early years; the range of augmentative and alternative communication options; and discusses the impact of literacy on articulation.

Children's Picture Books

Be Good to Eddie Lee
Fleming, Virginia & Cooper, Floyd (ill). 1997, 32 pp. The Putnam Publishing Co.
Eddie Lee is a boy with Down syndrome. Christy discovers special things about Eddie Lee, when Eddie Lee follows Christy into the woods.

My Friend Isabelle
Woloson, Eliza, Gough, Bryan (Ill.) 2003, 28 pp. Woodbine House
Isabelle and Charlie are friends. They both like to draw, dance, read, play at the park and cry if their feelings are hurt. They are also different from each other. Isabelle has Down syndrome and Charlie doesn't. This book opens the door for young children to talk about differences and the world around them.

Our Brother Has Down's Syndrome: An Introduction for Children
Cairo, Shelley: Cairo, Jasmine, et al. 1991, 10 pp. Firefly Books, LTD.
In this book, two sisters tell about their experience with having a little brother who has Down's syndrome.

Russ and the Almost Perfect Day
Rickert, Janet E. & McGahan, Pete (ill). 2001, 24 pp. Woodbine House.
Russ, a student with Down syndrome, is having a perfect day until he realizes that the five-dollar bill he has found probably belongs to a classmate.

Russ and the Firehouse
Rickert, Janet E. & McGahan, Pete (ill). 2000, 24 pp. Woodbine House.
Russ, a five-year-old with down Syndrome, visits his uncle's firehouse and gets to help with the daily chores.

We'll Paint the Octopus Red
Stuve-Bodeen, Stephanie & DeVito, Pam (ill). 1998, 28 pp. Woodbine House.
Emma and her father discuss what they will do when the new baby arrives, but they adjust their expectations when he is born with Down syndrome.

Where's Chimpy?
Rabe, Bernice., Schmidt, Diane. 1988, 13 pp. Albert Whitman
Text and photographs in this book show Misty, a little girl with Down syndrome, and her father reviewing her day's activities in their search for her stuffed monkey.

Epilepsy

Websites

www.efa.org
> Epilepsy Foundation

www.epilepsynse.org.uk/pages/index/home/
> National Society for Epilepsy

Resource Books

A Guide to Understanding and Living with Epilepsy
Devinsky, Orrin. 1994, 345 pp. Davis F. A.
This book is an important and easy-to-understand resource for people with epilepsy and for their families. Both the newly diagnosed and those living with epilepsy will find valuable information on a wide range of medical, social, and legal issues.

Epilepsy: Practical and Easy-to-Follow Advice
Marshall, Fiona. 1999, 146 pp. Element Books.
This book looks at the effective treatments which can help reduce the intensity and frequency of seizures and increase control of a child's epilepsy. It also includes stress-management techniques and ways to help your child create a positive self-image.

Seizures and Epilepsy in Childhood: A Guide for Parents
Freeman, John M.; Pillas, Diana, J & Vining, Eileen P. 1997, 322 pp. John Hopkins University Press.
This guide provides parents with the latest information about diagnosis, treatment, and the possible side effects of treatments, as well as offering practical advice about medication, decision-making, and risk-taking, which are all part of being the parent of a child with epilepsy

The Epilepsy Handbook: The Practical Management of Seizures
Gumnit, Robert J. 1994, 2nd ed. 194 pp. Lippincott-Raven Publishers.
A useful reference which provides an explanation of seizures and epilepsy, as well as treatment options for children and infants with epilepsy.

Children's Picture Books

Taking Seizure Disorders to School: A Story About Epilepsy
Gosselin, Kim., Freedman, Moss (ill). 1998, 32 pp. Jayjo Books, L L C
This picture book helps children to understand the condition of epilepsy

Lee, The Rabbit with Epilepsy

Moss, Deborah M., Schwartz, Carol (ill). 1990, 32 pp. Woodbine House.
Lee is diagnosed as having epilepsy, but medicine to control her seizures reduces her worries as she learns she can still lead a normal life

Dotty the Dalmation Has Epilepsy

Tim Peters Company Incorporated (ed). 1996, 20pp. Tim Peters & Company Incorporated.
This delightful story is about Dotty the Dalmatian who discovers she has epilepsy. At first, Dotty feels embarrassed and afraid. Once she accepts and learns how to control her seizures, however, she helps firefighters save lives.

Fetal Alcohol Syndrome

Websites

www.nofas.org
> Nofas Home Page

www.taconic.net/seminars/fas02.html
> Facts about FAS/FAE

www.cdc.gov/ncbddd/fas/
> National center on birth defects and developmental disabilities

Resource Books

Born Substance Exposed, Educationally Vulnerable

Vicent, Lisbeth J., et al. 1991, 30 pp. Council for Exceptional Children.
This book examines what is known about the long-term effects of inutero exposure to alcohol and other drugs, as well as the educational implications of those effects

Children of Prenatal Substance Abuse

Sparks, Shirley N., 1993, 177 pp. Singular Publishing Group, Inc.
Information is provided on substance abuse, addiction, biological and environmental risk factors, and physiological, mental health, and social outcomes. The author presents implications for working with families, including the effects of prenatal cocaine exposure on early childhood development, and assessment and intervention strategies for children affected by cocaine as infants, toddlers, and preschoolers. Also presented are the effects of maternal alcohol use during pregnancy and effective interventions for children with fetal alcohol syndrome or fetal alcohol effects.

Fantastic Antone Succeeds

Kleinfeld, Judith., Wescott, Siobhan. 1996, 368 pp. University of Alaska Press.

This book brings together experienced teachers, professionals, and parents to explore the issue of how to educate the alcohol-affected children whose numbers appear to be increasing in the schools and what parents can do at home and educators can do in the schools.

Teaching Children Affected by Prenatal Drug Exposure

Seitz de Martinez, Barbara J. (Ed). 1995, 323 pp. Phi Delta Kappa Intl, Inc.

The purpose of this book is to provide educators with a useful discussion of the facts and issues surrounding drug-exposed children in hope of facilitating a better understanding of these children and appropriate responses to their needs.

The Broken Cord

Dorris, Michael. 1989, 281 pp. Harper Collins Publishers Incorporated.

This is a story of a problem that is all around us today, fetal alcohol syndrome and fetal alcohol effects. It is a story of one family's life with a child of FAS. The book tries to open everyone's eyes to the completely preventable tragedy of children born with FAS and FAE.

What You Can Do to Prevent Fetal Alcohol Syndrome: A Professional's Guide

Blume, Sheila B. 1992, 58 pp. Hazelden Information and Educational Services.

This guide is designed to help professionals motivate clients to seek out early and adequate prenatal care, avoid all use of alcohol during pregnancy, explore ways to get help for alcohol and alcohol-related problems, and make the birth of their babies a happy event.

Fragile X Syndrome

Websites

www.fraxsocal.org
> What is Fragile X?

www.fraxa.org
> FRAXA Research Foundation - Fragile X

www.nfxf.org
> The National Fragile X Foundation - Fragile X Syndrome

Resource Books

Children with Fragile X Syndrome
Weber, Jayne D. (ed). 2000, 460 pp. Woodbine House.
This book is the first of its kind and provides parents with a conclusive, informative guide to Fragile X Syndrome

Fragile X Syndrome: A Guide for Teachers
Saunders, Suzanne. 2001, 128 pp. 1st Ed., David Fulton, Publishers.
Fragile X Syndrome is thought to be the most common inherited cause of learning difficulties. However, many people have never heard of it and those who have, including many of the professionals who work with those affected by it, have little knowledge or understanding of the condition. This book brings up-to-date research, information, and advice from teachers who are discovering, firsthand, the best ways of educating children with Fragile X.

Hunter Syndrome

Websites

members. aol.com/mpssociety/hunter.html
   MPS II - Hunter Syndrome

www.ggc.org/Diagnostics/Molecular/hunter_syndrome.htm
   Greenwood Genetic Center – Hunter Syndrome

Klinefelter Syndrome

Websites

www.aaksis.org
   American Association for Klinefelter Syndrome Information and Support

http://47xxy.org/
   Disease information, treatment descriptions and other links for Klinefelter
   Syndrome.

Resource Book

**The Official Parent's Sourcebook on Klinefelter Syndrome: A Revised and Updated
Directory for the Internet Age**
Icon Health Publications, 2002, 156 pp.
This book provides parents, caregivers, and other health professionals where and how to
look for information covering virtually all topics related to Klinefelter syndrome from the
essentials to the most advanced areas of research. Abundant references to reliable
internet-based resources are provided throughout the book. Where ever possible
guidance is provided on how to obtain free-of-charge material.

Learning Disabilities

Websites

www.ldonline.org
LD Online: Learning Disabilities Information & Resources

www.ldanatl.org
Learning Disabilities Association of America

www.ncld.org
National Center for Learning Disabilities

www.nimh.nih.gov/healthinformation/adhdmenu.cfm
Learning Disabilities

www.dyslexia.com
Information and Resources for Dyslexia

Resource Books

Dyslexia Action Plans for Success
Hannell, Glynis. 2004, 126 pp. Peytral Publications, Inc.
Based on current research this book provides a comprehensive overview of dyslexia and includes hundreds of practical action plans based on best practice. The book also includes teaching tips to help educators get through the major stumbling blocks experienced by students with dyslexia. The book covers reading, language, writing, spelling, math memory, concentration, motivation and more.

Educational Care: A System for Understanding and Helping Children with Learning Problems at Home and in School.
Levine, Melvin D. 1998, 325 pp. Educators Publishing Service, Incorporated.
This book provides useful strategies to try with students with disabilities to help them experience success in school.

Learning Disabilities: A to Z
Smith, Corinne., Strick, Lisa. 1999, 407 pp. Simon and Schuster Trade.
This book offers answers for parents of children who have neurological impairments affecting visual perception, language processing, fine motor skills, and the ability to focus attention.

Reflections on Dyslexia
LeMessurier, M., Sprod, R (filmmaker). 2005. Approximate 25 minutes
This is an excellent video to help promote awareness of dyslexia for teachers, parents and students. This video (or DVD) invites you to enter the world of a person with dyslexia,

to learn what has helped them and what has hindered their progress. The participants discuss the emotional issues behind dyslexia and how it has influenced their behaviors, opportunities and life choices. Filmed in Australia.

The School Survival Guide for Kids with LD: Ways to Make Learning Easier and More Fun.

Cummings, Rhoda., Fisher, Gary., Espeland, Pamela (ed.) 1991, 164 pp. Free Spirit Publishing, Inc.
This book will help answer questions for students with learning disabilities. It offers strategies and tips for building confidence in reading, writing, spelling, and math, managing time, coping with tests, and getting help. It also discusses how children with "learning differences" can get along better in school.

The Survival Guide for Kids with LD

Fisher, Gary L., Cummings, Rhoda., Nielsen, Nancy, J. (ed)., Urbanovic, Jackie (ill). 1991, 96 pp. Free Spirit Publishing, Inc.
This is a useful handbook for kids with learning disabilities. The book discusses different types of disorders, programs at school, coping with negative feelings, and making friends. It also includes a section for parents and teachers

Winning the Study Game – Learning How to Succeed in School

Greene, Lawrence. 2004 Peytral Publications, Inc.
Exceptional study skills program to help students improve reading comprehension, identify important information, memorize key facts, prepare for tests, take notes, manage time and more. These books are appropriate for students in grades 6-10 with a readability level of 5.5. The student book is also available in a consumable format.

Children's Picture Books

He's My Brother

Lasker, Joe. 1974, 38 pp. Albert Whitman.
A young boy describes the experiences of his slow-learning younger brother at school and at home

The Don't-Give-Up Kid and Learning Differences

Gehret, Jeanne. 1996, 3rd ed., 40 pp. Verbal Images Press.
As Alex becomes aware of his different learning style, he realizes that his hero Thomas Edison had similar problems.

Mental Retardation

Websites

www.thearc.org
> The Arc of the U.S. web site

www.cdc.gov/ncbddd/dd/ddmr.htm
> What is Mental Retardation?

Resource Books

Teaching Students with Mental Retardation: A Life-Goal Curriculum Planning Approach
Thomas, Glen E. 1996, 597 pp. Prentice Hall
This book provides information regarding students with mental impairments and offers ideas to use when planning curriculum.

When Slow is Fast Enough: Educating the Delayed Preschool Child
Goodman, Joan F. 1995, 306 pp. Guilford Publications, Inc.
The author of this book offers a less directive model of instruction in which the educator's aim is to support the child's natural and spontaneous, albeit slow, development, and to stimulate individual processes of discovery and self-expression.

Mental Retardation: Nature, Cause and Management
Baroff, George., Olley, Gregory. 1999, (3rd ed) 497 pp. Brunner/Mazel Publishers.
This book is a new edition revisiting the major issues affecting individuals with mental retardation, those responsible for their education and well-being, and society at large. This book includes up-to-date information on the disorder and its management.

Children with Mental Retardation
Smith, Romayne, M.A. 1993, 437 pp. Woodbine House
This is a book for parents of children with mental retardation. It provides positive insight and information regarding their child's medical, therapeutic, and educational needs. It gives parents an outlook they need to assist their child in reaching his or her highest potential.

Muscular Dystrophy

Websites

www.mdausa.org
> Muscular Dystrophy Association (MDA) USA homepage

www.mdff.org
> Muscular Dystrophy Family Foundation

www.mdausa.org/disease/index
> Muscular Dystrophy Association/ Disease

Resource Books

Muscular Dystrophy: The Facts
Emery, Alan E. H. 2000, 166 pp. 2nd ed. Oxford University Press, Incorporated.
This book will answer many of the questions that are often asked about how and why it occurs, and how it will affect the life of a recently diagnosed child.

Muscular Dystrophy in Children: A Guide for Families
Siegle, Irwin M. 1999, 130 pp. Demos Medical Publishing Incorporated.
This book is written for parents, friends, and educators of children who live with muscular dystrophy. It discusses common signs and symptoms and looks into the current treatment options available.

Children's Picture Books

Martin the Hero Merriweather
Jackson, Bobby; Carter, Michael; & Fultz, Jim (ill). 1993, 49 pp. Multicultural Publ.
Because of his physical handicap, Martin struggles to gain acceptance from his classmates, but he finally proves to the whole community that even he can be a hero

My Buddy
Osofsky, Audrey, Rand, Ted (ill). 1995, 54 pp. Houghton Mifflin Company.
A young boy with MD tells how he is teamed up with a dog trained to do things for him that he cannot do himself

Schizophrenia

Websites

www.schizophrenia.com
The Schizophrenia Home Page

www.pslgroup.com/SCHIZOPHR.htm
Schizophrenia - Doctor's Guide to the Internet

www.childadvocate.net/childhood_schizophrenia_summary.htm
Childhood Schizophrenia

Resource Books

Childhood Schizophrenia
Cantor, Sheila. 1998, 193 pp. Guildford Publications, Inc.
This book presents 54 case histories of schizophrenic children and reveals the family histories that show increased prevalence in these families of other neuropsychiatric disorders, such as epilepsy and mental retardation. The physical characteristics associated with childhood schizophrenia are described.

Coping with Schizophrenia: A Guide for Families
Mueser, Kim T., Gingerich, Susan. 1994, 355 pp. New Harbinger Publications.
This book provides helpful strategies for coping with stress and other issues related to schizophrenia.

I Am Not Sick, I Don't Need Help!
Amador, Xavier., Johanson, Anna-Lica. 2000, 240 pp. Vida Press.
This book explains in simplistic language how a family can work with their family member who is struggling with a mental illness. The author translates the research on mental illness into a highly readable and very practical book

Seasonal Affective Disorders

Websites

www.mentalhealth.com/book/p40-sad.html
> Seasonal Affective Disorder

www.athealth.com/Practitioner/Newsletter/FPN_3_2.html
> Seasonal Affective Disorder – SAD

www.bio-light.com
> Light Therapy for Seasonal Affective Disorder (SAD), Winter Depression: Light

Resource Books

Banishing the Blues of Seasonal Affective Disorder
Barr, Bruce C. 2000, 64 pp. Indoorsun.com Publishing.
This publication is a very clear and easy-to-read book about Seasonal Affective Disorder. This book provides information regarding the diagnosis for this condition as well as treatment plans available. Partial treatment focuses on using bright light therapy for the successful treatment of SAD.

Seasonal Affective Disorder: Who Gets It, What Causes It, How to Cure It
Smythe, Angela., Thompson, Chris. 1992, 288 pp. Thorsons Publishers
This book discusses treatment methods for SAD, or winter depression, used in clinics and describes how increased exposure to light helps sufferers experience a major mood change and energy rise

Winter Blues: Seasonal Affective Disorder: What It Is and How to Overcome It
Rosenthal, Norman E. 1998, 354 pp. Guilford Publications, Inc.
Information is provided on the dimensions of SAD. The book includes a self-test to help you evaluate your own level of SAD, as well as information regarding treatment of and coping with SAD

Spina Bifida

Websites

www.fortunecity.com/millenium/plumpton/268/sb.htm
        Information on spina bifida

www.nichcy.org/pubs/factshe/fs12txt.htm
        Spina Bifida Fact Sheet

www.sbadv.org
        Spina Bifida Home Page

Resource Books

Children with Spina Bifida: A Parent's Guide
Lutkenhof, Marlene (ed). 1999, 395 pp. Woodbine House.
This book is a very informative text for parents of special children with spina bifida.
This book provides information in an easy-to-understand and supportive way.

Spinabilities: A Young Person's Guide to Spina Bifida
Lutkenhof, Marlene (ed). 1997, 138 pp. Woodbine House.
This informative publication offers practical, no-nonsense advice for teenagers with spina bifida. This book will help teens manage their daily and long-term healthcare, tips on sex and relationships, and smart strategies for success at school and on the job, now ad down the road.

Teaching the Student with Spina Bifida
Rowley-Kelly, Fern L. (ed). Reigel, Donald H. (ed). 1992, 470 pp. Paul H. Brookes.
This book explores the aspects of social, personal, and cognitive development in students with spina bifida.

Children's Picture Book

Patrick and Emma Lou
Holcomb, Nan., Yoder, Dot (ill). 1992, 32 pp. Jason and Nordic Publishers.
Despite his excitement over walking with a new walker, three-year-old Patrick finds it isn't easy and becomes discouraged until his new friend, six-year-old Emma Lou who has spina bifida, helps him discover something important about himself.

Traumatic Brain Injury

Websites

www.neuroskills.com/index.html
Traumatic Brain Injury Resource Guide

www.tbiguide.com
Traumatic Brain Injury

www.biausa.org
Brain Injury Association USA Home Page

Resource Books

Coping with Mild Traumatic Brain Injury
Stoler, Diane R., Hill, Barbara, A. 1998, 334 pp. Avery Publishing Group, Inc.
Using clear, easy-to-understand language, the authors look at how the brain works and how it can be injured. They also discuss the procedures used to diagnose brain injuries, and the different treatments available.

Childhood Traumatic Brain Injury: Diagnosis, Assessment and Intervention
Bigler, Erin D. (Ed); Clark, Elaine (Ed); & Farmer, Janet, E. (Ed). 1997, 342 pp. Pro-Ed.
This resource provides information regarding the diagnosis of TBI, the assessment used to determine severity and effective intervention techniques to use with children with TBI.

Children with Traumatic Brain Injury
Schoenbrodt, Lisa (Ed). 2001, 350 pp. Woodbine House
This reference for parents provides support and information to help children recover from a traumatic brain injury. The resource is also useful to professionals who work with those with TBI and their families.

Traumatic Brain Injury in Children and Adolescents
Tyler, Janet S., Mira, Mary P. 1999, 149 pp. Pro-Ed, Incorporated.
This is a sourcebook providing information for teachers and other school personnel when working with children and adolescents with TBI.

Section VI

Disability Fact Sheets

The following material is provided courtesy of

National Information Center for Children and Youth with Disabilities (NICHCY).

National Information Center
for Children and Youth
with Disabilities

NICHCY

P.O. Box 1492
Washington, DC
20013-1492
E-Mail: nichcy@aed.org
Web: www.nichcy.org
1.800.695.0285 (V/TTY)

Autism/PDD

✦ Definition ✦

Autism and Pervasive Developmental Disorder-NOS (not otherwise specified) are developmental disabilities that share many of the same characteristics. Usually evident by age three, autism and PDD-NOS are neurological disorders that affect a child's ability to communicate, understand language, play, and relate to others.

In the diagnostic manual used to classify disabilities, the *DSM-IV* (American Psychiatric Association, 2000), "autistic disorder" is listed as a category under the heading of "Pervasive Developmental Disorders." A diagnosis of autistic disorder is made when an individual displays 6 or more of 12 symptoms listed across three major areas: social interaction, communication, and behavior. When children display similar behaviors but do not meet the criteria for autistic disorder, they may receive a diagnosis of Pervasive Developmental Disorder-NOS (PDD not otherwise specified). Although the diagnosis is referred to as PDD-NOS, throughout the remainder of this fact sheet, we will refer to the diagnosis as PDD, as it is more commonly known.

Autistic disorder is one of the disabilities specifically defined in the Individuals with Disabilities Education Act (IDEA), the federal legislation under which children and youth with disabilities receive special education and related services. IDEA, which uses the term "autism," defines the disorder as "a developmental disability significantly affecting verbal and nonverbal communication and social interaction, usually evident before age 3, that adversely affects a child's educational performance. Other characteristics often associated with autism are engagement in repetitive activities and stereotyped movements, resistance to environmental change or change in daily routines, and unusual responses to sensory experiences." (In keeping with the IDEA and the way in which this disorder is generally referred to in the field, we will use the term autism throughout the rest of this fact sheet.)

Due to the similarity of behaviors associated with autism and PDD, use of the term pervasive developmental disorder has caused some confusion among parents and professionals. However, the treatment and educational needs are similar for both diagnoses.

✦ Incidence ✦

Autism and PDD occur in approximately 5 to 15 per 10,000 births. These disorders are four times more common in boys than in girls.

The causes of autism and PDD are unknown. Currently, researchers are investigating areas such as neurological damage and biochemical imbalance in the brain. These disorders are not caused by psychological factors.

✦ Characteristics ✦

Some or all of the following characteristics may be observed in mild to severe forms:

- Communication problems (e.g., using and understanding language);

- Difficulty relating to people, objects, and events;

- Unusual play with toys and other objects;

- Difficulty with changes in routine or familiar surroundings; and

- Repetitive body movements or behavior patterns.

Children with autism or PDD vary widely in abilities, intelligence, and behaviors. Some children do not speak; others have language that often includes repeated phrases or conversations. Persons with more advanced language skills tend to use a small range of topics and have difficulty with abstract concepts. Repetitive play skills, a limited range of interests, and impaired social skills are generally evident as well. Unusual responses to sensory information—for example, loud noises, lights, certain textures of food or fabrics—are also common.

✦ Educational Implications ✦

Early diagnosis and appropriate educational programs are very important to children with autism or PDD. Public Law (P.L.) 105-17, the Individuals with Disabilities Education Act (IDEA), formerly P.L. 94-142, includes autism as a disability category. From the age of three, children with autism and PDD are eligible for an educational program appropriate to their individual needs. Educational programs for students with autism or PDD focus on improving communication, social, academic, behavioral, and daily living skills. Behavior and communication problems that interfere with learning sometimes require the assistance of a knowledgeable professional in the autism field who develops and helps to implement a plan which can be carried out at home and school.

The classroom environment should be structured so that the program is consistent and predictable. Students with autism or PDD learn better and are less confused when information is presented visually as well as verbally. Interaction with nondisabled peers is also important, for these students provide models of appropriate language, social, and behavioral skills. To overcome frequent problems in generalizing skills learned at school, it is very important to develop programs with parents, so that learning activities, experiences, and approaches can be carried over into the home and community.

With educational programs designed to meet a student's individual needs and specialized adult support services in employment and living arrangements, children and adults with autism or PDD can live and work in the community.

✦ Resources ✦

Bondy, A., & Frost, L. (2002). *A picture's worth: PECS and other visual communication strategies in autism.* Bethesda, MD: Woodbine House. (Telephone: 800-843-7323. Web: www.woodbinehouse.com)

Harris, S. (1994). *Siblings of children with autism: A guide for families.* Bethesda, MD: Woodbine House. (See contact information above.)

Harris, S.L., & Weiss, M.J. (1998). *Right from the start: Behavioral intervention for young children with autism: A guide for parents and professionals.* Bethesda, MD: Woodbine House. (See contact information above.)

Journal of Autism and Developmental Disorders. (Available from Kluwer Academic Publishers at 781-871-6600. Web: www.wkap.nl/)

Maurice, C., Green, G., & Luce, S.C. (Eds.). (1996). *Behavioral intervention for young children with autism: A manual for parents and professionals.* Austin, TX: Pro-Ed. (Telephone: 800-897-3202. Web: www.proedinc.com)

McClannaham, L.E., & Krantz, P.J. (1999). *Activity schedules for children with autism: Teaching independent behavior.* Bethesda, MD: Woodbine House. (See contact information above.)

Powers, M.D. (Ed.). (2000). *Children with autism: A parent's guide* (2nd ed.). Bethesda, MD: Woodbine House. (See contact information above.)

Richman, S. (2001). *Raising a child with autism: A guide to applied behavior analysis for parents.* London: Jessica Kingsley Publishers. (Web: www.jkp.com/)

Schopler, E., & Mesibov, G.B. (Eds.). Books available in the "Current Issues in Autism" book series include: *Behavioral issues in autism* (1995); *Learning and cognition in autism* (1995); *Asperger syndrome or high-functioning autism?* (1998); *The research basis for autism intervention* (2001); *Understanding Asperger syndrome and high functioning autism* (2001). (All are available from Kluwer Academic Publishers at 781-871-6600. Web: www.wkap.nl/)

✦ Organizations ✦

Autism Hotline
Autism Services Center
P.O. Box 507, Huntington, WV 25710-0507
304-525-8014
Web: www.autismservices.com

Autism National Committee
P.O. Box 6175, North Plymouth, MA 02362-6175
Web: www.autcom.org

Autism Society of America
7910 Woodmont Avenue, Suite 300
Bethesda, MD 20814
301-657-0881; 800-328-8476
Email: info@autism-society.org
Web: www.autism-society.org

Indiana Resource Center for Autism
Indiana Institute on Disability and Community
2853 East 10th Street, Indiana University
Bloomington, IN 47408-2696
812-855-6508; 812-855-9396 (TTY)
Web: www.iidc.indiana.edu/~irca

IDEAs that Work
U.S. Office of Special Education Program:

FS1, January 2003

Publication of this document is made possible through Cooperative Agreement #H326N980002 between the Academy for Educational Development and the Office of Special Education Programs of the U.S. Department of Education. The contents of this document do not necessarily reflect the views or policies of the Department of Education, nor does mention of trade names, commercial products, or organizations imply endorsement by the U.S. Government.

Deafness & Hearing Loss

NICHCY Disability Fact Sheet—No. 3

✧ Definition ✧

The Individuals with Disabilities Education Act (IDEA), formerly the Education of the Handicapped Act (P.L. 94-142), includes "hearing impairment" and "deafness" as two of the categories under which children with disabilities may be eligible for special education and related services programming. While the term "hearing impairment" is often used generically to describe a wide range of hearing losses, including deafness, the regulations for IDEA define hearing loss and deafness separately.

Hearing impairment is defined by IDEA as "an impairment in hearing, whether permanent or fluctuating, that adversely affects a child's educational performance."

Deafness is defined as "a hearing impairment that is so severe that the child is impaired in processing linguistic information through hearing, with or without amplification."

Thus, deafness may be viewed as a condition that prevents an individual from receiving sound in all or most of its forms. In contrast, a child with a hearing loss can generally respond to auditory stimuli, including speech.

✧ Incidence ✧

Hearing loss and deafness affect individuals of all ages and may occur at any time from infancy through old age. The U.S. Department of Education (2002) reports that during the 2000-2001 school year, 70,767 students aged 6 to 21 (or 1.3% of all students with disabilities) received special education services under the category of "hearing impairment." However, the number of children with hearing loss and deaf-

NICHCY *is the*
National Dissemination Center for Children with Disabilities.

NICHCY
P.O. Box 1492
Washington, DC 20013
1.800.695.0285 (Voice / TTY)
202.884.8200 (Voice / TTY)
nichcy@aed.org
www.nichcy.org

ness is undoubtedly higher, since many of these students may have other disabilities as well and may be served under other categories.

✧ Characteristics ✧

It is useful to know that sound is measured by its loudness or intensity (measured in units called decibels, dB) and its frequency or pitch (measured in units called hertz, Hz). Impairments in hearing can occur in either or both areas, and may exist in only one ear or in both ears. Hearing loss is generally described as slight, mild, moderate, severe, or profound, depending upon how well a person can hear the intensities or frequencies most greatly associated with speech. Generally, only children whose hearing loss is greater than 90 decibels (dB) are considered deaf for the purposes of educational placement.

There are four types of hearing loss. *Conductive* hearing losses are caused by diseases or obstructions in the outer or middle ear (the conduction pathways for sound to reach the inner ear). Conductive hearing losses usually affect all frequencies of hearing evenly and do not result in severe losses. A person with a conductive hearing loss usually is able to use a hearing aid well or can be helped medically or surgically.

Sensorineural hearing losses result from damage to the delicate sensory hair cells of the inner ear or the nerves which supply it. These hearing losses can range from mild to profound. They often affect the person's ability to hear certain frequencies more than others. Thus, even with amplification to increase the sound level, a person with a sensorineural hearing loss may perceive distorted sounds, sometimes making the successful use of a hearing aid impossible.

A *mixed* hearing loss refers to a combination of conductive and senso-rineural loss and means that a problem occurs in both the outer or middle and the inner ear. A *central* hearing loss results from damage or impairment to the nerves or nuclei of the central nervous system, either in the pathways to the brain or in the brain itself.

Don't Be Shy!

All of our publications and resource lists are online—help yourself! Visit us at:

www.nichcy.org

If you'd like personalized assistance, email or call us:

nichcy@aed.org

1.800.695.0285 (V/TTY)

✧ Educational Implications ✧

Hearing loss or deafness does not affect a person's intellectual capacity or ability to learn. However, children who are either hard of hearing or deaf generally require some form of special education services in order to receive an adequate education. Such services may include:

- regular speech, language, and auditory training from a specialist;

- amplification systems;

- services of an interpreter for those students who use sign language;

- favorable seating in the class to facilitate lip reading;

- captioned films/videos;

- assistance of a notetaker, who takes notes for the student with a hearing loss, so that the student can fully attend to instruction;

- instruction for the teacher and peers in alternate communication methods, such as sign language; and

- counseling.

Children who are hard of hearing will find it much more difficult than children who have normal hearing to learn vocabulary, grammar, word order, idiomatic expressions, and other aspects of verbal communication. For children who are deaf or have severe hearing losses, early, consistent, and conscious use of visible communication modes (such as sign language, fingerspelling, and Cued Speech) and/or amplification and aural/oral training can help reduce this language delay. By age four or five, most children who are deaf are enrolled in school on a full-day basis and do special work on communication and language development. It is important for teachers and audiologists to work together to teach the child to use his or her residual hearing to the maximum extent possible, even if the preferred means of communication is manual. Since the great majority of deaf children (over 90%) are born to hearing parents, programs should provide instruction for parents on implications of deafness within the family.

Other Helpful Things to Know

These NICHCY publications talk about topics important to parents of a child with a disability.

Parenting a Child with Special Needs

Your Child's Evaluation

Parent to Parent Support

Questions Often Asked by Parents About Special Education Services

Developing Your Child's IEP

All are available in English and in Spanish—on our Web site or by contacting us.

Hearing loss or deafness does not affect a person's intellectual capacity or ability to learn.

People with hearing loss use oral or manual means of communication or a combination of the two. Oral communication includes speech, lip reading, and the use of residual hearing. Manual communication involves signs and fingerspelling. Total Communication, as a method of instruction, is a combination of the oral method plus signing and fingerspelling.

Individuals with hearing loss, including those who are deaf, now have many helpful devices available to them. *Text telephones* (known as TTs, TTYs, or TDDs) enable persons to type phone messages over the telephone network. The *Telecommunications Relay Service* (TRS) makes it possible for TT users to communicate with virtually anyone (and vice versa) via telephone. Dial 711 to access all TRSs anywhere in the United States. The relay service is free.

✧ Resources ✧

Luterman, D.M. (2002). *When your child is deaf: A guide for parents* (2nd ed.). Parkton, MD: York Press. (Phone: 800.962.2763. Web: www.yorkpress.com/index.html)

Medwid, D.J., & Weston, D.C. (1995). *Kid-friendly parenting with deaf and hard of hearing children: A treasury of fun activities toward better behavior.* Washington, DC: Gallaudet University Press. (Phone: 800.621.2736; 888.630.9347 (V/TTY). Web: http://gupress.gallaudet.edu)

Ogden, P.W. (1996). *The silent garden: Raising your deaf child* (Rev. ed.). Washington, DC: Gallaudet University Press. (See contact information above.)

Schwartz, S. (Ed.). (1996). *Choices in deafness: A parents' guide to communication options* (2nd ed.). Bethesda, MD: Woodbine House. (Phone: 800.843.7323. Web: www.woodbinehouse.com)

So your child has a hearing loss: Next steps for parents (n.d.). (Available online at: www.agbell.org/information/brochures_parent_so.cfm)

✧ Organizations ✧

Alexander Graham Bell Association
for the Deaf and Hard of Hearing
3417 Volta Place, NW, Washington, DC 20007
202.337.5220; 202.337.5221 (TTY)
info@agbell.org
www.agbell.org

American Society for Deaf Children
P.O. Box 3355, Gettysburg, PA 17325
717.334.7922 (V/TTY); 800.942.2732 (V/TTY)
ASDC1@aol.com
www.deafchildren.org

American Speech-Language-Hearing Association
10801 Rockville Pike, Rockville, MD 20852
301.897.5700 (V/TTY)
800.638.8255 (V/TTY)
www.asha.org

Laurent Clerc National Deaf Education Center
KDES PAS-6, Gallaudet University
800 Florida Avenue N.E.
Washington, DC 20002-3695
202.651.5051 (V/TTY)
Clearinghouse.InfoToGo@gallaudet.edu
http://clerccenter.gallaudet.edu/InfoToGo

National Institute on Deafness and Other
Communication Disorders Information
Clearinghouse
1 Communication Avenue
Bethesda, MD 20892-3456
800.241.1044; 800.241.1055 (TTY)
nidcdinfo@nidcd.nih.gov
www.nidcd.nih.gov/

Self Help for Hard of Hearing People (SHHH)
7910 Woodmont Avenue, Suite 1200
Bethesda, MD 20814
301.657.2248; 301.657.2249 (TTY)
info@hearingloss.org
www.hearingloss.org

FS3, January 2004

IDEAs that Work
U.S. Office of Special
Education Programs

Publication of this document is made possible through Cooperative Agreement #H326N030003 between the Academy for Educational Development and the Office of Special Education Programs of the U.S. Department of Education. The contents of this document do not necessarily reflect the views or policies of the Department of Education, nor does mention of trade names, commercial products, or organizations imply endorsement by the U.S. Government.

Down Syndrome

✧ Definition ✧

Down syndrome is the most common and readily identifiable chromosomal condition associated with mental retardation. It is caused by a chromosomal abnormality: for some unexplained reason, an accident in cell development results in 47 instead of the usual 46 chromosomes. This extra chromosome changes the orderly development of the body and brain. In most cases, the diagnosis of Down syndrome is made according to results from a chromosome test administered shortly after birth.

✧ Incidence ✧

Approximately 4,000 children with Down syndrome are born in the U.S. each year, or about 1 in every 800 to 1,000 live births. Although parents of any age may have a child with Down syndrome, the incidence is higher for women over 35. Most common forms of the syndrome do not usually occur more than once in a family.

✧ Characteristics ✧

There are over 50 clinical signs of Down syndrome, but it is rare to find all or even most of them in one person. Some common characteristics include:

- Poor muscle tone;

- Slanting eyes with folds of skin at the inner corners (called epicanthal folds);

- Hyperflexibility (excessive ability to extend the joints);

- Short, broad hands with a single crease across the palm on one or both hands;

NICHCY *is the National Dissemination Center for Children with Disabilities.*

*NICHCY
P.O. Box 1492
Washington, DC 20013
1.800.695.0285 (Voice / TTY)
202.884.8200 (Voice / TTY)
nichcy@aed.org
www.nichcy.org*

- Broad feet with short toes;

- Flat bridge of the nose;

- Short, low-set ears;

- Short neck;

- Small head;

- Small oral cavity; and/or

- Short, high-pitched cries in infancy.

Individuals with Down syndrome are usually smaller than their nondisabled peers, and their physical as well as intellectual development is slower.

Besides having a distinct physical appearance, children with Down syndrome frequently have specific health-related problems. A lowered resistance to infection makes these children more prone to respiratory problems. Visual problems such as crossed eyes and far- or nearsightedness are higher in individuals with Down syndrome, as are mild to moderate hearing loss and speech difficulty.

Approximately one third of babies born with Down syndrome have heart defects, most of which are now successfully correctable. Some individuals are born with gastrointestinal tract problems that can be surgically corrected.

Some people with Down syndrome also may have a condition known as Atlantoaxial Instability, a misalignment of the top two vertebrae of the neck. This condition makes these indi-viduals more prone to injury if they participate in activities which overex-tend or flex the neck. Parents are urged to have their child examined by a physician to determine whether or not their child should be restricted from sports and activities which place stress on the neck. Although this misalignment is a potentially serious condition, proper diagnosis can help prevent serious injury.

Don't Be Shy!

All of our publications and resource lists are online— help yourself! Visit us at:

www.nichcy.org

If you'd like personalized assistance, email or call us:

nichcy@aed.org

1.800.695.0285
(V/TTY)

Children with Down syndrome may have a tendency to become obese as they grow older. Besides having negative social implications, this weight gain threatens these individuals' health and longevity. A supervised diet and exercise program may help reduce this problem.

✧ Educational Implications ✧

Shortly after a diagnosis of Down syndrome is confirmed, parents should be encouraged to enroll their child in an infant development/early intervention program. These programs offer parents special instruction in teaching their child language, cognitive, self-help, and social skills, and specific exercises for gross and fine motor development. Research has shown that stimulation during early developmental stages improves a child's chances of developing to his or her fullest potential. Continuing education, positive public attitudes, and a stimulating home environment have also been found to promote the child's overall development.

Just as in the normal population, there is a wide variation in mental abilities, behavior, and developmental progress in individuals with Down syndrome. Their level of retardation may range from mild to severe, with the majority functioning in the mild to moderate range. Due to these individual differences, it is impossible to predict future achievements of children with Down syndrome.

Because of the range of ability in children with Down syndrome, it is important for families and all members of the school's education team to place few limitations on potential capabilities. It may be effective to emphasize concrete concepts rather than abstract ideas. Teaching tasks in a step-by-step manner with frequent reinforcement and consistent feedback has proven successful. Improved public acceptance of persons with disabilities, along with increased opportunities for adults with disabilities to live and work independently in the community, have expanded goals for individuals with Down syndrome. Independent Living Centers, group-

Other Helpful Things to Know

These NICHCY publications talk about topics important to parents of a child with a disability.

Parenting a Child with Special Needs

Your Child's Evaluation

Parent to Parent Support

Questions Often Asked by Parents About Special Education Services

Developing Your Child's IEP

All are available in English and in Spanish—on our Web site or by contacting us.

Research has shown that stimulation during early developmental stages improves a child's chances of developing to his or her fullest potential.

shared and supervised apartments, and support services in the community have proven to be important resources for persons with disabilities.

✧ Resources ✧

Cunningham, C. (1999). *Understanding Down syndrome: An introduction for parents* (2nd ed.). Cambridge, MA: Brookline. (Phone: 800.666.2665. Web: www.brooklinebooks.com)

Pueschel, S.M. (Ed.). (2001). *A parent's guide to Down syndrome: Toward a brighter future* (2nd ed.). Baltimore, MD: Paul H. Brookes. (Phone: 800.638.3775. Web: www.brookespublishing.com)

Unruh, J.F. (1994). *Down syndrome: Successful parenting of children with Down syndrome.* Eugene, OR: Fern Ridge Press. (Phone: 800.816.5679. Web: www.fernridgepress.com/)

Woodbine House (Phone: 800.843.7323, Web: www.woodbinehouse.com) publishes a series on Down syndrome, including:

- *Babies with Down syndrome: A new parent's guide*

- *Differences in common: Straight talk about mental retardation, Down syndrome, and life*

- *Down syndrome: The first 18 months (DVD or Video)*

- *Early Communication skills in children with Down syndrome: A guide for parents and professionals*

- *Fine motor skills in children with Down syndrome*

- *Gross motor skills in children with Down syndrome*

- *Medical and surgical care for children with Down syndrome: A guide for parents*

- *Teaching reading to children with Down syndrome*

✧ Organizations ✧

National Down Syndrome Congress
1370 Center Drive, Suite 102
Atlanta, GA 30338
770.604.9500; 800.232.6372
info@ndsccenter.org
www.ndsccenter.org

National Down Syndrome Society
666 Broadway
New York, NY 10012
212.460.9330; 800.221.4602
info@ndss.org
ndss.org

The Arc of the United States
1010 Wayne Avenue, Suite 650
Silver Springs, MD 20910
301.565.3842
info@thearc.org
www.thearc.org

FS4, January 2004

Publication of this document is made possible through Cooperative Agreement #H326N030003 between the Academy for Educational Development and the Office of Special Education Programs of the U.S. Department of Education. The contents of this document do not necessarily reflect the views or policies of the Department of Education, nor does mention of trade names, commercial products, or organizations imply endorsement by the U.S. Government.

Emotional Disturbance

✧ Definition ✧

Many terms are used to describe emotional, behavioral, or mental disorders. Currently, students with such conditions are categorized as having an emotional disturbance, which is defined under the Individuals with Disabilities Education Act (IDEA) as follows:

"...a condition exhibiting one or more of the following characteristics over a long period of time and to a marked degree that adversely affects a child's educational performance—

(A) An inability to learn that cannot be explained by intellectual, sensory, or health factors.

(B) An inability to build or maintain satisfactory interpersonal relationships with peers and teachers.

(C) Inappropriate types of behavior or feelings under normal circumstances.

(D) A general pervasive mood of unhappiness or depression.

(E) A tendency to develop physical symptoms or fears associated with personal or school problems." *[Code of Federal Regulations*, Title 34, §300.7(c)(4)(i)]

As defined by IDEA at §300.7(c)(4)(ii), emotional disturbance includes schizophrenia but does not apply to children who are socially maladjusted, unless it is determined that they have an emotional disturbance.

NICHCY *is the National Dissemination Center for Children with Disabilities.*

NICHCY
P.O. Box 1492
Washington, DC 20013
1.800.695.0285 (Voice / TTY)
202.884.8200 (Voice / TTY)
nichcy@aed.org
www.nichcy.org

✧ Incidence ✧

In the 2000-2001 school year, 473,663 children and youth with emotional disturbance were provided special education and related services in the public schools (*Twenty-fourth Annual Report to Congress*, U.S. Department of Education, 2002).

✧ Characteristics ✧

The causes of emotional disturbance have not been adequately determined. Although various factors such as heredity, brain disorder, diet, stress, and family functioning have been suggested as possible causes, research has not shown any of these factors to be the direct cause of behavior or emotional problems. Some of the characteristics and behaviors seen in children who have emotional disturbances include:

- Hyperactivity (short attention span, impulsiveness);

- Aggression/self-injurious behavior (acting out, fighting);

- Withdrawal (failure to initiate interaction with others, retreat from exchanges or social interaction, excessive fear or anxiety);

- Immaturity (inappropriate crying, temper tantrums, poor coping skills); and

- Learning difficulties (academically performing below grade level).

Children with the most serious emotional disturbances may exhibit distorted thinking, excessive anxiety, bizarre motor acts, and abnormal mood swings. Some are identified as children who have severe psychosis or schizophrenia.

Many children who do not have emotional disturbance may display some of these same behaviors at various times during their development. However, when children have an emotional disturbance, these behaviors continue over long periods of time. Their behavior signals that they are not coping with their environment or peers.

Don't Be Shy!

All of our publications and resource lists are online—help yourself! Visit us at:

www.nichcy.org

If you'd like personalized assistance, email or call us:

nichcy@aed.org

1.800.695.0285 (V/TTY)

✧ Educational Implications ✧

The educational programs for children with an emotional disturbance need to include attention to providing emotional and behavioral support as well as helping them to master academics, develop social skills, and increase self-awareness, self-control, and self-esteem. A large body of research exists regarding methods of providing students with positive behavioral support (PBS) in the school environment, so that problem behaviors are minimized and positive, appropriate behaviors are fostered. (See the resource list at the end of this publication for more information on PBS.) It is also important to know that, within the school setting:

- For a child whose behavior impedes learning (including the learning of others), the team developing the child's Individualized Education Program (IEP) needs to consider, if appropriate, strategies to address that behavior, including positive behavioral interventions, strategies, and supports.

- Students eligible for special education services under the category of emotional disturbance may have IEPs that include psychological or counseling services. These are important related services which are available under law and are to be provided by a qualified social worker, psychologist, guidance counselor, or other qualified personnel.

- Career education (both vocational and academic) is also a major part of secondary education and should be a part of the transition plan included in every adolescent's IEP.

There is growing recognition that families, as well as their children, need support, respite care, intensive case management, and a collaborative, multi-agency approach to services. Many communities are working toward providing these wrap-around services. There are a growing number of agencies and organizations actively involved in establishing support services in the community.

Other Helpful Things to Know

These NICHCY publications talk about topics important to parents of a child with a disability.

Parenting a Child with Special Needs

Your Child's Evaluation

Parent to Parent Support

Questions Often Asked by Parents About Special Education Services

Developing Your Child's IEP

All are available in English and in Spanish—on our Web site or by contacting us.

A large body of research exists regarding methods of providing students with positive behavioral support (PBS) in the school environment.

✦ Other Considerations ✦

Families of children with an emotional disturbance may need help in understanding their children's condition and in learning how to work effectively with them. Parent support groups can be helpful in this regard. Organizations such as the National Mental Health Association (NMHA) and the National Alliance for the Mentally Ill (NAMI) have parent groups in every state. (See "Organizations.") Help is also available from psychiatrists, psychologists, or other mental health professionals in public or private mental health settings. Children should be provided services based on their individual needs, and all persons who are involved with these children should be aware of the care they are receiving. It is important to coordinate all services between home, school, and therapeutic community with open communication.

✦ Resources ✦

Greene, R.W. (2001). *The explosive child: A new approach for understanding and parenting easily frustrated chronically inflexible children.* New York: Harper Collins. (Phone: 212.207.7000. Web: www.harpercollins.com/hc/home.asp)

Jordan, D. (2001). *A guidebook for parents of children with emotional or behavior disorders* (3rd ed.). Minneapolis, MN: PACER. (Phone: 888.248.0822. Web: www.pacer.org)

Koplewicz, H.S. (1997). *It's nobody's fault: New hope and help for difficult children.* New York: Three Rivers Press. (To find a local or online bookseller, go to: www.randomhouse.com/reader_resources/ordering.html)

Miller, J.A. (1999). *The childhood depression sourcebook.* New York: McGraw-Hill. (Phone: 877.833.5524. Web: http://books.mcgraw-hill.com)

Papolos, D., & Papolos, J. (2002). *The bipolar child.* New York: Broadway. (To find a local or online bookseller, go to: www.randomhouse.com/reader_resources/ordering.html)

Wilen, T.E. (1998). *Straight talk about psychiatric medications for kids.* New York: Guilford. (Phone: 800.365.7006. Web: www.guilford.com)

✦ Organizations ✦

American Academy of Child and Adolescent Psychiatry, Public Information Office
3615 Wisconsin Ave., NW
Washington, DC 20016-3007
202.966.7300
www.aacap.org

Center on Positive Behavioral Interventions and Supports
5262 University of Oregon
Eugene, OR 97403-5262
541.346.2505
pbis@oregon.uregon.edu
www.pbis.org

Federation of Families for Children's Mental Health, 1101 King Street, Suite 420
Alexandria, VA 22314
703.684.7710
ffcmh@ffcmh.org
www.ffcmh.org

National Alliance for the Mentally Ill (NAMI)
Colonial Place Three, 2107 Wilson Boulevard, Suite 300, Arlington, VA 22201-3042
703.524.7600; 703.516.7227 (TTY)
800.950.6264
www.nami.org

National Mental Health Association
2001 N. Beauregard St., 12th Floor
Alexandria, VA 22311
703.684.7722; 800.969.6642
800.433.5959 (TTY)
www.nmha.org

National Mental Health Information Center
P.O. Box 42557
Washington, DC 20015
800.789.2647; 866.889.2647 (TTY)
www.mentalhealth.org

FS5, January 2004

IDEAs that Work
U.S. Office of Special Education Programs

AED ·

Publication of this document is made possible through Cooperative Agreement #H326N030003 between the Academy for Educational Development and the Office of Special Education Programs of the U.S. Department of Education. The contents of this document do not necessarily reflect the views or policies of the Department of Education, nor does mention of trade names, commercial products, or organizations imply endorsement by the U.S. Government.

Epilepsy

✧ Definition ✧

According to the Epilepsy Foundation of America, epilepsy is a physical condition that occurs when there is a sudden, brief change in how the brain works. When brain cells are not working properly, a person's consciousness, movement, or actions may be altered for a short time. These physical changes are called epileptic seizures. Epilepsy is therefore sometimes called a seizure disorder. Epilepsy affects people in all nations and of all races.

Some people can experience a seizure and not have epilepsy. For example, many young children have convulsions from fevers. These febrile convulsions are one type of seizure. Other types of seizures not classified as epilepsy include those caused by an imbalance of body fluids or chemicals or by alcohol or drug withdrawal. A single seizure does not mean that the person has epilepsy.

✧ Incidence ✧

About two million Americans have epilepsy; of the 125,000 new cases that develop each year, up to 50% are in children and adolescents.

✧ Characteristics ✧

Although the symptoms listed below are not necessarily indicators of epilepsy, it is wise to consult a doctor if you or a member of your family experiences one or more of them:

- "Blackouts" or periods of confused memory;

- Episodes of staring or unexplained periods of unresponsiveness;

NICHCY *is the*
National Dissemination Center for Children with Disabilities.

NICHCY
P.O. Box 1492
Washington, DC 20013
1.800.695.0285 (Voice / TTY)
202.884.8200 (Voice / TTY)
nichcy@aed.org
www.nichcy.org

- Involuntary movement of arms and legs;

- "Fainting spells" with incontinence or followed by excessive fatigue; or

- Odd sounds, distorted perceptions, episodic feelings of fear that cannot be explained.

Seizures can be generalized, meaning that all brain cells are involved. One type of generalized seizure consists of a convulsion with a complete loss of consciousness. Another type looks like a brief period of fixed staring.

Seizures are partial when those brain cells not working properly are limited to one part of the brain. Such partial seizures may cause periods of "automatic behavior" and altered consciousness. This is typified by purposeful-looking behavior, such as buttoning or unbuttoning a shirt. Such behavior, however, is unconscious, may be repetitive, and is usually not recalled.

✧ Educational Implications ✧

Students with epilepsy or seizure disorders are eligible for special education and related services under the Individuals with Disabilities Education Act (IDEA). Epilepsy is classified as "other health impaired" and an Individualized Education Program (IEP) would be developed to specify appropriate services. Some students may have additional conditions such as learning disabilities along with the seizure disorders.

Seizures may interfere with the child's ability to learn. If the student has the type of seizure characterized by a brief period of fixed staring, he or she may be missing parts of what the teacher is saying. It is important that the teacher observe and document these episodes and report them promptly to parents and to school nurses.

Don't Be Shy!

All of our publications and resource lists are online— help yourself! Visit us at:

www.nichcy.org

If you'd like personalized assistance, email or call us:

nichcy@aed.org

1.800.695.0285 (V/TTY)

Depending on the type of seizure or how often they occur, some children may need additional assistance to help them keep up with classmates. Assistance can include adaptations in classroom instruction, first aid instruction on seizure management to the student's teachers, and counseling, all of which should be written in the IEP.

It is important that the teachers and school staff are informed about the child's condition, possible effects of medication, and what to do in case a seizure occurs at school. Most parents find that a friendly conversation with the teacher(s) at the beginning of the school year is the best way to handle the situation. Even if a child has seizures that are largely controlled by medication, it is still best to notify the school staff about the condition.

School personnel and the family should work together to monitor the effectiveness of medication as well as any side effects. If a child's physical or intellectual skills seem to change, it is important to tell the doctor. There may also be associated hearing or perception problems caused by the brain changes. Written observations of both the family and school staff will be helpful in discussions with the child's doctor.

Children and youth with epilepsy must also deal with the psychological and social aspects of the condition. These include public misperceptions and fear of seizures, uncertain occurrence, loss of self control during the seizure episode, and compliance with medications. To help children feel more confident about themselves and accept their epilepsy, the school can assist by providing epilepsy education programs for staff and students, including information on seizure recognition and first aid.

Students can benefit the most when both the family and school are working together. There are many materials available for families and teachers so that they can understand how to work most effectively as a team.

Other Helpful Things to Know

These NICHCY publications talk about topics important to parents of a child with a disability.

Parenting a Child with Special Needs

Your Child's Evaluation

Parent to Parent Support

Questions Often Asked by Parents About Special Education Services

Developing Your Child's IEP

All are available in English and in Spanish—on our Web site or by contacting us.

Students with epilepsy or seizure disorders are eligible for special education and related services under IDEA.

✧ Resources ✧

Epilepsy Foundation of America. (n.d.). *Epilepsy: Questions and answers about seizure disorders*. Landover, MD: Author. (See address below.)

Freeman, J.M., Vining, E.P.G., & Pillas, D.J. (2003). *Seizures and epilepsy in childhood: A guide for parents* (3rd ed.). Baltimore, MD: Johns Hopkins University Press. (Phone: 800.537.5487. Web: www.press.jhu.edu/books/index.html)

Lechtenberg, R. (2002). *Epilepsy and the family: A new guide* (2nd ed.). Cambridge, MA: Harvard University Press. (Phone: 800.448.2242. Web: www.hup.harvard.edu)

✧ Organizations ✧

Epilepsy Foundation—National Office
4351 Garden City Drive
Landover, MD 20785-7223
301.459.3700; 800.332.1000
301.577.0100 (For publications)
www.epilepsyfoundation.org

National Institute of Neurological Disorders and Stroke (NINDS)
National Institutes of Health
P.O. Box 5801
Bethesda, MD 20824
301.496.5751; 800.352.9424
www.ninds.nih.gov/

FS6, January 2004

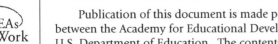

Publication of this document is made possible through Cooperative Agreement #H326N030003 between the Academy for Educational Development and the Office of Special Education Programs of the U.S. Department of Education. The contents of this document do not necessarily reflect the views or policies of the Department of Education, nor does mention of trade names, commercial products, or organizations imply endorsement by the U.S. Government.

This publication is copyright free. Readers are encouraged to copy and share it, but please credit NICHCY.

Spina Bifida

✧ Definition ✧

Spina Bifida means cleft spine, which is an incomplete closure in the spinal column. In general, the three types of spina bifida (from mild to severe) are:

Spina Bifida Occulta: There is an opening in one or more of the vertebrae (bones) of the spinal column without apparent damage to the spinal cord.

Meningocele: The meninges, or protective covering around the spinal cord, has pushed out through the opening in the vertebrae in a sac called the "meningocele." However, the spinal cord remains intact. This form can be repaired with little or no damage to the nerve pathways.

Myelomeningocele: This is the most severe form of spina bifida, in which a portion of the spinal cord itself protrudes through the back. In some cases, sacs are covered with skin; in others, tissue and nerves are exposed. Generally, people use the terms "spina bifida" and "myelomeningocele" interchangeably.

✧ Incidence ✧

Approximately 40% of all Americans may have spina bifida occulta, but because they experience little or no symptoms, very few of them ever know that they have it. The other two types of spina bifida, meningocele and myelomeningocele, are known collectively as "spina bifida manifesta," and occur in approximately one out of every thousand births. Of these infants born with

NICHCY *is the National Dissemination Center for Children with Disabilities.*

NICHCY
P.O. Box 1492
Washington, DC 20013
1.800.695.0285 (Voice / TTY)
202.884.8200 (Voice / TTY)
nichcy@aed.org
www.nichcy.org

"spina bifida manifesta," about 4% have the meningocele form, while about 96% have myelomeningocele form.

✧ Characteristics ✧

The effects of myelomeningocele, the most serious form of spina bifida, may include muscle weakness or paralysis below the area of the spine where the incomplete closure (or cleft) occurs, loss of sensation below the cleft, and loss of bowel and bladder control. In addition, fluid may build up and cause an accumulation of fluid in the brain (a condition known as hydrocephalus). A large percentage (70%-90%) of children born with myelomeningocele have hydrocephalus. Hydrocephalus is controlled by a surgical procedure called "shunting," which relieves the fluid buildup in the brain. If a drain (shunt) is not implanted, the pressure buildup can cause brain damage, seizures, or blindness. Hydrocephalus may occur without spina bifida, but the two conditions often occur together.

✧ Educational Implications ✧

Although spina bifida is relatively common, until recently most children born with a myelomeningocele died shortly after birth. Now that surgery to drain spinal fluid and protect children against hydrocephalus can be performed in the first 48 hours of life, children with myelomeningocele are much more likely to live. Quite often, however, they must have a series of operations throughout their childhood. School programs should be flexible to accommodate these special needs.

Many children with myelomeningocele need training to learn to manage their bowel and bladder functions. Some require catheterization, or the insertion of a tube to permit passage of urine.

Don't Be Shy!

All of our publications and resource lists are online— help yourself! Visit us at:

www.nichcy.org

If you'd like personalized assistance, email or call us:

nichcy@aed.org

1.800.695.0285 (V/TTY)

The courts have held that clean, intermittent catheterization is necessary to help the child benefit from and have access to special education and related services. A successful bladder management program can be incorporated into the regular school day. Many children learn to catheterize themselves at a very early age.

In some cases, children with spina bifida who also have a history of hydrocephalus experience learning problems. They may have difficulty with paying attention, expressing or understanding language, and grasping reading and math. Early intervention with children who experience learning problems can help considerably to prepare them for school.

Successful integration of a child with spina bifida into school sometimes requires changes in school equipment or the curriculum. In adapting the school setting for the child with spina bifida, architectural factors should be considered. Section 504 of the Rehabilitation Act of 1973 requires that programs receiving federal funds make their facilities accessible. This can occur through structural changes (for example, adding elevators or ramps) or through schedule or location changes (for example, offering a course on the ground floor).

Children with myelomeningocele need to learn mobility skills, and often require the aid of crutches, braces, or wheelchairs. It is important that all members of the school team and the parents understand the child's physical capabilities and limitations. Physical disabilities like spina bifida can have profound effects on a child's emotional and social development. To promote personal growth, families and teachers should encourage children, within the limits of safety and health, to be independent and to participate in activities with their nondisabled classmates.

Other Helpful Things to Know

These NICHCY publications talk about topics important to parents of a child with a disability.

Parenting a Child with Special Needs

Your Child's Evaluation

Parent to Parent Support

Questions Often Asked by Parents About Special Education Services

Developing Your Child's IEP

All are available in English and in Spanish— on our Web site or by contacting us.

In some cases, children with spina bifida who also have a history of hydrocephalus, experience learning problems.

✧ Resources ✧

Lutkenhoff, M. (Ed.). (1999). *Children with spina bifida: A parents' guide.* Bethesda, MD: Woodbine House. (Phone: 800.843.7323. Web: www.woodbinehouse.com)

Lutkenhoff, M., & Oppenheimer, S. (1997). *SPINAbilities: A young person's guide to spina bifida.* Bethesda, MD: Woodbine House. (See contact information above.)

National Institute of Neurological Disorders and Stroke (NINDS). (2001). NINDS spina bifida information page. Available online at: www.ninds.nih.gov/health_and_medical/disorders/spina_bifida.htm

Sandler, A. (1997). *Living with spina bifida: A guide for families and professionals.* Chapel Hill, NC: University of North Carolina Press. (Phone: 800.848.6224. Web: uncpress.unc.edu/)

Spina Bifida Association of America. (n.d.). *Facts about spina bifida.* Washington, DC: Author. (See "Organizations." Available online at: www.sbaa.org/html/sbaa_facts.html)

✧ Organizations ✧

Spina Bifida Association of America
4590 MacArthur Boulevard, N.W., Suite 250
Washington, DC 20007-4226
202.944.3285
800.621.3141
sbaa@sbaa.org
www.sbaa.org

March of Dimes Birth Defects Foundation
1275 Mamaroneck Avenue
White Plains, NY 10605
914.428.7100
888.663.4637
askus@marchofdimes.com
www.marchofdimes.com

Easter Seals—National Office
230 West Monroe Street, Suite 1800
Chicago, IL 60606
312.726.6200; 312.726.425 (TTY)
800.221.6827
info@easter-seals.org
www.easter-seals.org

National Rehabilitation Information Center (NARIC)
4200 Forbes Boulevard, Suite 202
Lanham, MD 20706
301.459.5900; 301.459.5984 (TTY)
800.346.2742
naricinfo@heitechservices.com
www.naric.com

FS12, January 2004

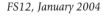

Publication of this document is made possible through Cooperative Agreement #H326N030003 between the Academy for Educational Development and the Office of Special Education Programs of the U.S. Department of Education. The contents of this document do not necessarily reflect the views or policies of the Department of Education, nor does mention of trade names, commercial products, or organizations imply endorsement by the U.S. Government.

Speech & Language Impairments

✧ Definition ✧

Speech and language disorders refer to problems in communication and related areas such as oral motor function. These delays and disorders range from simple sound substitutions to the inability to understand or use language or use the oral-motor mechanism for functional speech and feeding. Some causes of speech and language disorders include hearing loss, neurological disorders, brain injury, mental retardation, drug abuse, physical impairments such as cleft lip or palate, and vocal abuse or misuse. Frequently, however, the cause is unknown.

✧ Incidence ✧

More than one million of the students served in the public schools' special education programs in the 2000-2001 school year were categorized as having a speech or language impairment. This estimate does not include children who have speech/language problems secondary to other conditions such as deafness. Language disorders may be related to other disabilities such as mental retardation, autism, or cerebral palsy. It is estimated that communication disorders (including speech, language, and hearing disorders) affect one of every 10 people in the United States.

✧ Characteristics ✧

A child's communication is considered delayed when the child is noticeably behind his or her peers in the acquisition of speech and/or language skills. Sometimes a child will have greater receptive (understanding) than expressive (speaking) language skills, but this is not always the case.

NICHCY *is the National Dissemination Center for Children with Disabilities.*

NICHCY
P.O. Box 1492
Washington, DC 20013
1.800.695.0285 (Voice / TTY)
202.884.8200 (Voice / TTY)
nichcy@aed.org
www.nichcy.org

Speech disorders refer to difficulties producing speech sounds or problems with voice quality. They might be characterized by an interruption in the flow or rhythm of speech, such as stuttering, which is called dysfluency. Speech disorders may be problems with the way sounds are formed, called articulation or phonological disorders, or they may be difficulties with the pitch, volume, or quality of the voice. There may be a combination of several problems. People with speech disorders have trouble using some speech sounds, which can also be a symptom of a delay. They may say "see" when they mean "ski" or they may have trouble using other sounds like "l" or "r." Listeners may have trouble understanding what someone with a speech disorder is trying to say. People with voice disorders may have trouble with the way their voices sound.

A language disorder is an impairment in the ability to understand and/or use words in context, both verbally and nonverbally. Some characteristics of language disorders include improper use of words and their meanings, inability to express ideas, inappropriate grammatical patterns, reduced vocabulary, and inability to follow directions. One or a combination of these characteristics may occur in children who are affected by language learning disabilities or developmental language delay. Children may hear or see a word but not be able to understand its meaning. They may have trouble getting others to understand what they are trying to communicate.

✧ Educational Implications ✧

Because all communication disorders carry the potential to isolate individuals from their social and educational surroundings, it is essential to find appropriate timely intervention. While many speech and language patterns can be called "baby talk" and are part of a young child's normal development, they

can become problems if they are not outgrown as expected. In this way an initial delay in speech and language or an initial speech pattern can become a disorder that can cause difficulties in learning. Because of the way the brain develops, it is easier to learn language and communication skills before the age of 5. When children have muscular disorders, hearing problems, or developmental delays, their acquisition of speech, language, and related skills is often affected.

Speech-language pathologists assist children who have communication disorders in various ways. They provide individual therapy for the child; consult with the child's teacher about the most effective ways to facilitate the child's communication in the class setting; and work closely with the family to develop goals and techniques for effective therapy in class and at home. The speech-language pathologist may assist vocational teachers and counselors in establishing communication goals related to the work experiences of students and suggest strategies that are effective for the important transition from school to employment and adult life.

Technology can help children whose physical conditions make communication difficult. The use of electronic communication systems allow nonspeaking people and people with severe physical disabilities to engage in the give and take of shared thought.

Vocabulary and concept growth continues during the years children are in school. Reading and writing are taught and, as students get older, the understanding and use of language becomes more complex. Communication skills are at the heart of the education experience. Speech and/or language therapy may continue throughout a student's school years either in the form of direct therapy or on a consultant basis.

Other Helpful Things to Know

These NICHCY publications talk about topics important to parents of a child with a disability.

Parenting a Child with Special Needs

Your Child's Evaluation

Parent to Parent Support

Questions Often Asked by Parents About Special Education Services

Developing Your Child's IEP

All are available in English and in Spanish—on our Web site or by contacting us.

Because of the way the brain develops, it is easier to learn language and communication skills before the age of 5.

✧ Resources ✧

Brice, A. (2001). *Children with communication disorders* (ERIC Digest #E617). Arlington, VA: ERIC Clearinghouse on Disabilities and Gifted Education. (Available online at: http://ericec.org/digests/e617.html)

Charkins, H. (1996). *Children with facial differences: A parents' guide.* Bethesda, MD: Woodbine House. (Phone: 800.843.7323. Web: www.woodbinehouse.com)

Cleft Palate Foundation. (1997). *For parents of newborn babies with cleft lip/cleft palate.* Chapel Hill, NC: Author. (Phone: 800.242.5338. Also available online at: www.cleftline.org)

Gruman-Trinker, C. (2001). *Your cleft-affected child: The complete book of information, resources and hope.* Alameda, CA: Hunter House. (Web: www.hunterhouse.com)

Hamaguchi, P.M. (2001). *Childhood speech, language, and listening problems: What every parent should know* (2nd ed.). New York: John Wiley. (Phone: 800.225.5945. Web: www.wiley.com/)

✧ Organizations ✧

Alliance for Technology Access
2175 E. Francisco Blvd., Suite L
San Rafael, CA 94901
415.455.4575; 800.455.7970
atainfo@ataccess.org
www.ataccess.org

American Speech-Language-Hearing Association (ASHA)
10801 Rockville Pike, Rockville, MD 20852
301.897.5700 (V/TTY); 800.638.8255
actioncenter@asha.org
www.asha.org

Childhood Apraxia of Speech Association of North America (CASANA)
123 Eisele Road, Cheswick, PA 15024
412.767.6589
helpdesk@apraxia.org
www.apraxia-kids.org

Cleft Palate Foundation
104 South Estes Drive, Suite 204
Chapel Hill, NC 27514
919.933.9044; 800.242.5338
info@cleftline.org
www.cleftline.org

Easter Seals—National Office
230 West Monroe Street, Suite 1800
Chicago, IL 60606
312.726.6200; 312.726.4258 (TTY);
800.221.6827
info@easter-seals.org
www.easter-seals.org

Learning Disabilities Association of America (LDA)
4156 Library Road
Pittsburgh, PA 15234-1349
412.341.1515
info@ldaamerica.org
www.ldaamerica.org

Scottish Rite Foundation
Southern Jurisdiction, U.S.A., Inc.
1733 Sixteenth Street, N.W.
Washington, DC 20009
202.232.3579.
www.srmason-sj.org/web/index.htm

Trace Research and Development Center
University of Wisconsin- Madison
1550 Engineering Dr.
2107 Engineering Hall
Madison, WI 53706
608.262.6966; 608.263.5408 (TTY)
info@trace.wisc.edu
www.trace.wisc.edu

FS11, January 2004

Publication of this document is made possible through Cooperative Agreement #H326N030003 between the Academy for Educational Development and the Office of Special Education Programs of the U.S. Department of Education. The contents of this document do not necessarily reflect the views or policies of the Department of Education, nor does mention of trade names, commercial products, or organizations imply endorsement by the U.S. Government.

Visual Impairments

✧ Definition ✧

The terms partially sighted, low vision, legally blind, and totally blind are used in the educational context to describe students with visual impairments. These terms are defined as follows:

- "Partially sighted" indicates some type of visual problem has resulted in a need for special education;

- "Low vision" generally refers to a severe visual impairment, not necessarily limited to distance vision. Low vision applies to all individuals with sight who are unable to read the newspaper at a normal viewing distance, even with the aid of eyeglasses or contact lenses. They use a combination of vision and other senses to learn, although they may require adaptations in lighting, the size of print, and, sometimes, braille;

- "Legally blind" indicates that a person has less than 20/200 vision in the better eye or a very limited field of vision (20 degrees at its widest point); and

- Totally blind students, who learn via braille or other non-visual media.

Visual impairment is the consequence of a functional loss of vision, rather than the eye disorder itself. Eye disorders which can lead to visual impairments can include retinal degeneration, albinism, cataracts, glaucoma, muscular problems that result in visual disturbances, corneal disorders, diabetic retinopathy, congenital disorders, and infection.

NICHCY *is the*
National Dissemination Center
for Children with Disabilities.

NICHCY
P.O. Box 1492
Washington, DC 20013
1.800.695.0285 (Voice / TTY)
202.884.8200 (Voice / TTY)
nichcy@aed.org
www.nichcy.org

✧ Incidence ✧

The rate at which visual impairments occur in individuals under the age of 18 is 12.2 per 1,000. Severe visual impairments (legally or totally blind) occur at a rate of .06 per 1,000.

✧ Characteristics ✧

The effect of visual problems on a child's development depends on the severity, type of loss, age at which the condition appears, and overall functioning level of the child. Many children who have multiple disabilities may also have visual impairments resulting in motor, cognitive, and/or social developmental delays.

A young child with visual impairments has little reason to explore interesting objects in the environment and, thus, may miss opportunities to have experiences and to learn. This lack of exploration may continue until learning becomes motivating or until intervention begins.

Because the child cannot see parents or peers, he or she may be unable to imitate social behavior or under-stand nonverbal cues. Visual disabilities can create obstacles to a growing child's independence.

✧ Educational Implications ✧

Children with visual impairments should be assessed early to benefit from early intervention programs, when applicable. Technology in the form of computers and low-vision optical and video aids enable many partially sighted, low vision, and blind children to participate in regular class activities. Large print materials, books on tape, and braille books are available.

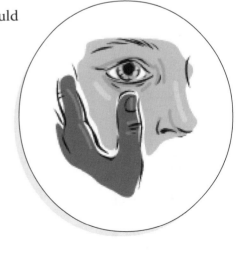

Don't Be Shy!

All of our publications and resource lists are online—help yourself! Visit us at:

www.nichcy.org

If you'd like personalized assistance, email or call us:

nichcy@aed.org

1.800.695.0285 (V/TTY)

Students with visual impairments may need additional help with special equipment and modifications in the regular curriculum to emphasize listening skills, communication, orientation and mobility, vocation/career options, and daily living skills. Students with low vision or those who are legally blind may need help in using their residual vision more efficiently and in working with special aids and materials. Students who have visual impairments combined with other types of disabilities have a greater need for an interdisciplinary approach and may require greater emphasis on self care and daily living skills.

✧ Resources ✧

American Foundation for the Blind. Search AFB's *Service Center* on the Internet to identify services for blind and visually impaired persons in the United States and Canada. Available: www.afb.org/services.asp

Holbrook, M.C. (Ed.). (1996). *Children with visual impairments: A parents' guide.* Bethesda, MD: Woodbine. (Phone: 800.843.7323. Web: www.woodbinehouse.com)

Lewis, S., & Allman, C.B. (2000). *Seeing eye to eye: An administrator's guide to students with low vision.* New York: American Foundation for the Blind. (Phone: 800.232.3044. Web: www.afb.org)

National Eye Institute. (2003, December). *Eye health organizations list.* (Available online at: www.nei.nih.gov/health/organizations.htm)

Other Helpful Things to Know

These NICHCY publications talk about topics important to parents of a child with a disability.

Parenting a Child with Special Needs

Your Child's Evaluation

Parent to Parent Support

Questions Often Asked by Parents About Special Education Services

Developing Your Child's IEP

All are available in English and in Spanish— on our Web site or by contacting us.

The terms partially sighted, low vision, legally blind, and totally blind are used in the educational context to describe students with visual impairments.

✧ Organizations ✧

American Council of the Blind
1155 15th St. N.W., Suite 1004
Washington, D.C. 20005
202.467.5081; 800.424.8666
info@acb.org
www.acb.org

American Foundation for the Blind
11 Penn Plaza, Suite 300
New York, NY 10001
800.232.5463 (Hotline)
For publications call: 800.232.3044
afbinfo@afb.net
www.afb.org

Blind Children's Center
4120 Marathon Street
Los Angeles, CA 90029-0159
323.664.2153; 800.222.3566
info@blindchildrenscenter.org
www.blindchildrenscenter.org

National Association for Parents of
the Visually Impaired, Inc.
P.O. Box 317
Watertown, MA 02472-0317
617.972.7441; 800.562.6265
napvi@perkins.org
www.napvi.org

National Association for Visually
Handicapped
22 West 21st Street, 6th Floor
New York, NY 10010
212.889.3141
staff@navh.org
www.navh.org

National Braille Association, Inc. (NBA)
3 Townline Circle
Rochester, NY 14623-2513
585.427.8260
nbaoffice@nationalbraille.org
www.nationalbraille.org/

National Braille Press
88 St. Stephen Street
Boston, MA 02115
617.266.6160; 888.965.8965
orders@nbp.org
www.nbp.org

National Eye Institute
31 Center Drive
MSC 2510
Bethesda, MD 20892-2510
301.496.5248
2020@nei.nih.gov
www.nei.nih.gov

National Federation of the Blind,
Parents Division
1800 Johnson Street
Baltimore, MD 21230
410.659.9314, ext. 360
nfb@nfb.org
www.nfb.org/nopbc.htm

National Library Service for the Blind
and Physically Handicapped,
Library of Congress
1291 Taylor Street, N.W.
Washington, D.C. 20011
202.707.5100; 202.707.0744 (TTY);
800.424.8567
nls@loc.gov
www.loc.gov/nls

Prevent Blindness America
500 E. Remington Road
Schaumburg, IL 60173
847.843.2020; 800.331.2020
info@preventblindness.org
www.preventblindness.org

The Foundation Fighting Blindness
(formerly the National Retinitis
Pigmentosa Foundation)
11435 Cronhill Drive
Owings Mills, MD 21117-2220
410.568.0150; 410.363.7139 (TTY)
888.394.3937; 800.683.5551 (TTY)
info@blindness.org
www.blindness.org

FS13, January 2004

Publication of this document is made possible through Cooperative Agreement #H326N030003
between the Academy for Educational Development and the Office of Special Education Programs of the
U.S. Department of Education. The contents of this document do not necessarily reflect the views or policies
of the Department of Education, nor does mention of trade names, commercial products, or organizations
imply endorsement by the U.S. Government.

This publication is copyright free. Readers are encouraged to copy and share it, but please credit NICHCY.

Bibliography

Bender, W. N. (2003). *LearningDisabilities: Characteristics, Identification, and Teaching Strategies.* (5th ed.). Boston: Allyn and Bacon.

Canter, L., & Canter M. (1997). *Succeeding with Difficult Students.* Santa Monica, CA: Lee Canter & Associates.

Clayman, C. B. (Ed.). (1989). *The American Medical Association Encyclopedia of Medicine.* New York: Random House, Incorporated.

Dornbush, M. P. & Pruitt, S. K. (1995). *Teaching the Tiger: A Handbook for Individuals Involved in the Education of Students with Attention Deficit Disorders, Tourette Syndrome, or Obsessive-Compulsive Disorder.* Duarte, CA: Hope Press.

Dulcan, M. K., Lisarralde, C. (Eds.). (2002). *Helping Parents, Youth, and Teachers Understand Medications for Behavioral and Emotional Problems: A Resource Book of Medication Information Handouts.* (2nd ed.) Washington, DC: American Psychiatric Press.

Hammeken, P.A. (2003). *Inclusion: An Essential Guide for the Paraprofessional.* (2nd ed.) Minnetonka, MN: Peytral Publications, Inc.

Hammeken, P.A., (2000). *Inclusion: 450 Strategies for Success.* (2nd ed.) Minnetonka, MN: Peytral Publications, Inc.

Heward, W. L., Orlansky, M. D. (2002). *Exceptional Children.* (7th ed.). New York: Macmillan Publishing Company.

Kerr, M. M., Nelson, C. M. (1997). *Strategies for Managing Behavior Problems in the Classroom.* (3rd ed.). New York: Macmillan Publishing Company.

Kerr, M. M., Nelson, C. M., & Lambert, D. L. (1987). *Helping Adolescents with Learning and Behavior Problems.* Columbus, OH: Merrill Publishing Company.

McLoughlin, J. A., & Lewis, R. B. (2000). *Assessing Students with Special Needs..* (5th ed.). New York: Macmillan Publishing Company.

Mercer, C. D. & Mercer, A. R. (2000) *Teaching Students with Special Needs.* (6th ed.). New York: Macmillan Publishing Company.

Minnesota Department of Children, Families & Learning. (1996). *Total Special Education Systems (TSES) Generic Policies and Procedures Manual.* Little Canada, MN

Peirangelo, Roger Ph.D. (2003). *The Special Educator's Book of Lists.* San Francisco, CA: John Wiley and Sons, Inc.

Reif, S. F. (1993). *How to Reach and Teach ADD/ADHD Children.* New York: The Center for Applied Research in Education.

Silverman, Harold M. (2002). *The Pill Book.* (10th ed.). New York: Bantam Books.

Sugai, G. M., & Tindal, G. A. (1993). *Effective School Consultation: An Interactive Approach.* Pacific Grove, CA: Brooks/Cole Publishing Company.

Winebrenner, Susan. (1996) *Teaching Kids with Learning Difficulties in the Regular Classroom.* Minneapolis, MN: Free Spirit Publishing, Inc.

Yanoff, J.C. (2000). *The Classroom Teacher's Inclusion Handbook.* Chicago: Arthur Coyle Press

Subject Index